Mastering Business Structures

Your guide to choosing the right structure for your business, legal frameworks, profit maximizing, growth securing

Introduction

In today's fast-paced world, where entrepreneurship is more than a career choice—it's a calling, understanding the foundational aspects of starting a business is paramount. Among these, selecting an appropriate business structure stands out as a critical decision, one that can dictate the trajectory of your entrepreneurial journey. This decision, while seemingly straightforward, involves navigating a labyrinth of legal frameworks, tax implications, and operational complexities. It's here, at this crossroads of uncertainty and opportunity, that this book aims to be your compass.

We are DA Affiliates 2, business strategists with over eight years of experience guiding both budding startups and established enterprises through the maze of business optimization. Our journey has been one of passion, fueled by a genuine desire to see others succeed in the often tumultuous world of business. With a background that blends business management expertise with a relentless pursuit of entrepreneurial excellence, We've dedicated our career to demystifying the complexities of business structures for those who dare to dream.

"Mastering Business Structures" is more than a book; it's a mission to transform the overwhelming into the understandable, to convert apprehension into action. It's designed to equip you, the aspiring entrepreneur, with the knowledge and tools necessary to choose the business structure that best aligns with your vision. From dissecting legal frameworks to strategies for maximizing profits and securing growth, this book promises a journey of discovery and empowerment.

As we venture through each chapter, you'll be met with a blend of real-world examples, actionable advice, and interactive elements — all aimed at engaging you in a dialogue about your future. Whether it's understanding the nuances of a sole proprietorship or the complexities of a corporation, the insights shared here are meant to not only inform but inspire.

The essence of this book is to ensure that by the final page, you possess not just an understanding of business structures, but the confidence to choose the one that heralds the best future for your enterprise. We're tailoring this journey for beginners, breaking down barriers of jargon and complexity, making each step towards your business goals as clear and accessible as possible.

Our own story began with a simple desire: to make a difference in the lives of those brave enough to venture into entrepreneurship. Each challenge faced, and each victory earned, has reinforced my commitment to this cause. I share this journey with you not just as an author but as a fellow traveler on the path to business success.

As we embark on this journey together, I encourage you to approach each chapter with an open mind and a resolve to master the intricacies of business structures. The knowledge you'll gain here is more than academic; it's a cornerstone upon which you can build a thriving enterprise.

We invite you to connect with me on social

media,such as, Linkedin, Facebook, Instagram, and X specifically through DA Affiliates 2, where our conversation can continue. There, you'll find a community of like-minded individuals, additional resources, and ongoing support as you navigate the exciting world of entrepreneurship.

Together, let's step confidently into the future, armed with the knowledge and understanding to make informed decisions about the structure of your business.

Table of Contents

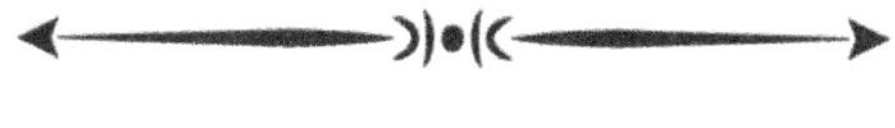

Chapter 1

In the realm of entrepreneurship, the choice of business structure holds a pivotal role, acting as the framework within which your venture will operate, grow, and potentially transform. This decision influences not only legal and financial aspects of your business but also its very identity and operational dynamics. The business structure you select will dictate your path through the complexities of taxation, liability, and decision-making authority. It's a decision that demands careful consideration, informed by a clear understanding of the options available and the implications each one holds.

1.1   Sole Proprietorships: Simplicity and Control

At the heart of the entrepreneurial spirit lies the sole proprietorship, the simplest and most straightforward form of business structure. It is characterized by the singularity of its ownership and operation, embodying the essence of entrepreneurial autonomy. This structure is notably appealing for its ease of formation, often requiring no formal action beyond the standard business licensing and registration with local authorities. The allure of the sole proprietorship lies in its simplicity; there are no partners, no board of directors, and no shareholders to dilute the owner's control or complicate decision-making processes. The autonomy of a sole proprietorship grants the owner unilateral control over all aspects of the business, from operational decisions to the allocation of resources. This control is a double-edged sword, offering unparalleled agility in business operations. Decisions can be made swiftly, without the need for consensus or consultation, allowing the business to adapt and respond to market changes with remarkable speed. However, this agility comes with the weight of full responsibility for the success or failure of the venture.

One of the most significant considerations for prospective sole proprietors is the issue of personal liability. Unlike corporations or limited liability companies (LLCs) where the business entity is separate from its owners, a sole proprietorship does not provide a legal distinction between the business and the individual. This means that the owner's personal assets — such as their home, car, and savings — are directly linked to the business liabilities. In practical terms, if the business incurs debt or faces legal action, the owner's personal assets could be at risk to satisfy business debts and liabilities.

Amidst these considerations, the taxation structure of sole proprietorships offers a semblance of simplicity in the complex world of business finance. Profits and losses from the business are reported directly on the owner's personal tax returns, streamlining the tax filing process. This direct reporting method, known as "pass-through" taxation, ensures that business income is taxed only once, at the individual's personal tax rate, avoiding the double taxation often associated with corporate structures. It's a feature that underscores the appeal of sole proprietorships for entrepreneurs eager to minimize their tax burden and simplify their financial management.

Reflecting on Sole Proprietorship

As you contemplate the prospect of establishing a sole proprietorship, consider your comfort level with assuming full responsibility for the business's liabilities. Reflect on the scale and scope of your venture, and whether the simplicity and control offered by a sole proprietorship align with your business goals and personal risk tolerance. This reflection is not merely an exercise in self-assessment but a fundamental step in laying the groundwork for a business structure that resonates with your aspirations and operational style.

In this context, the narrative of a local bookstore owner comes to mind, who, having opted for a sole proprietorship, found a harmonious balance between entrepreneurial independence and operational simplicity. The bookstore, nestled in the heart of the community, became a testament to the effectiveness of this structure in fostering close connections with customers and responding nimbly to the evolving landscape of local commerce. The owner's direct involvement in every facet of the business—from curating the collection to hosting community events—exemplified the unique advantages of sole proprietorship in creating a venture deeply intertwined with personal passion and community engagement.

The journey of choosing the right business structure is one of thoughtful consideration, informed by an understanding of the legal, financial, and operational implications. As you navigate this decision, let the simplicity and control of a sole proprietorship serve as a reference point, a reminder of the fundamental values that drive entrepreneurial endeavors. Whether you ultimately decide on a sole proprietorship or another structure, the key lies in aligning your choice with your vision, risk tolerance, and long-term goals, ensuring that the foundation you lay today supports the growth and success of your venture tomorrow.

1.2   The LLC: Flexibility and Protection

Within the tapestry of business structures, the Limited Liability Company (LLC) stands out as a beacon of flexibility and protection. It operates as a separate legal entity, much like a corporation, yet it offers a blend of benefits that cater to the nuanced needs of modern entrepreneurs. This dual nature of the LLC ensures that the personal assets of the owners, often referred to as members, remain distinct and shielded from the debts and liabilities of the business. Such a structure is a fortress around the personal wealth of the individuals involved, safeguarding homes, savings, and other assets from the reach of business creditors—a crucial consideration for anyone venturing into the unpredictable waters of entrepreneurship.

The allure of the LLC extends into the realm of taxation, where it presents a chameleon-like adaptability. By default, LLCs enjoy the benefits of pass-through taxation, a principle that allows business profits to flow directly to the members' personal tax returns, circumventing the specter of double taxation that haunts corporations. This pass-through status ensures that earnings are taxed only once, preserving the financial health of the business and its members. Yet, for those who find advantage in the corporate tax structure, the LLC offers the flexibility to elect corporate taxation, a choice that might suit certain financial strategies, particularly in businesses aiming to reinvest profits rather than distribute them immediately. This tax flexibility, rare in the landscape of business structures, empowers entrepreneurs to tailor their tax strategies to the evolving needs and opportunities of their ventures.

Operational freedom further characterizes the LLC, setting it apart from the more rigid frameworks of corporations. The absence of a mandated board of directors or annual meetings liberates LLC members from the procedural shackles that might constrain the agility of a corporation. This operational flexibility allows for a dynamic approach to management and decision-making, enabling members to structure their roles and responsibilities in a manner that aligns with the venture's strategic goals and the members' individual strengths. Such fluidity is particularly beneficial in rapidly changing markets, where the ability to pivot and adapt can be the difference between success and obsolescence.

Despite these advantages, the LLC is not without its complexities, particularly when it comes to the patchwork of state-specific regulations that govern its formation and operation. Each state in the U.S. has its own set of rules and requirements for LLCs, affecting everything from the paperwork necessary to establish the entity to the annual fees required to maintain good standing. These variations can influence the strategic advantages of forming an LLC, making some states more favorable than others depending on the specific needs and circumstances of the business. For instance, while one state may offer tax incentives that align with the goals of a particular LLC, another might impose burdensome reporting requirements or fees that detract from those benefits. As such, the decision to form an LLC — and where to do so — requires a careful analysis of state-specific regulations, a task that underscores the importance of due diligence and, often, professional guidance in navigating the legal landscape of business formation.

The narrative of an entrepreneur who leveraged the LLC structure to protect personal assets while enjoying tax flexibility exemplifies the strategic value of this choice. In this case, the business, a boutique marketing firm, faced the volatile tides of industry trends and client demands, a situation that called for both legal protection and operational agility. By forming an LLC, the owner not only shielded personal assets from potential liabilities but also capitalized on the pass-through taxation to optimize financial outcomes. The operational freedom inherent in the LLC structure allowed for a nimble response to market changes, empowering the firm to pivot its strategies without the encumbrance of corporate formalities. This strategic use of the LLC framework highlights its role not just as a protective measure, but as a platform for growth and adaptation in a competitive landscape.

In the end, the LLC stands as a testament to the evolving nature of business, offering a blend of protection, flexibility, and tax efficiency that resonates with the diverse needs of modern entrepreneurs. Its appeal lies not only in the safeguards it provides but in the freedom it offers, allowing businesses to navigate the complexities of the market with agility and strategic foresight. As such, the LLC represents a compelling option for those seeking a balance between the autonomy of sole proprietorship and the robust protections of a corporation, underscored by a tax structure that can be tailored to the financial strategies of the venture.

1.3   Partnerships: Collaboration with Care

In the landscape of business structures, partnerships emerge as entities that embody collaboration, pooling resources, expertise, and visions to forge ventures that may not be feasible for individuals working in isolation. This structure is inherently built on the foundation of mutual trust and shared objectives, yet it is diversified into several forms, each with its distinct characteristics and implications for the partners involved.

The general partnership, the archetype of this structure, operates under the principle of equal responsibility and authority. Here, each partner not only contributes to the business but also shares in the profits and bears the burden of losses and liabilities equally. This symmetry ensures a democratic approach to decision-making and operational management, fostering an environment of collective effort and reward. Yet, it also implies a shared vulnerability, as each partner's personal assets could be exposed to the business's liabilities, underscoring the importance of mutual respect and shared values among the partners.

Diverging from the egalitarian nature of general partnerships are limited partnerships, which introduce a hierarchy of roles between general and limited partners. General partners retain the authority and responsibility for managing the business, bearing the brunt of liabilities, while limited partners contribute capital without involving themselves in the day-to-day operations.

This division allows individuals to invest in the venture without exposing themselves to the operational risks and liabilities that general partners face. However, it also necessitates a clear delineation of roles and responsibilities, documented meticulously to avoid conflicts and ensure the smooth functioning of the partnership.

A further evolution in the partnership structure is seen in the limited liability partnership (LLP), a hybrid that offers each partner protection from the liabilities incurred by others. This structure is particularly appealing to professionals such as lawyers, accountants, and consultants, for whom the risk of malpractice or negligence by a partner could potentially endanger personal assets.

The LLP shields each partner's personal holdings from such exposures, providing a layer of security that enables the pursuit of professional practices within a collaborative framework. Yet, this protection also demands strict adherence to regulatory requirements, including registration and compliance with state-specific laws that govern LLPs.

The intricacies of partnerships extend into the realm of taxation, where the principle of pass-through taxation applies, mirroring the treatment seen in sole proprietorships and LLCs. Profits and losses are distributed among the partners according to the terms set forth in the partnership agreement, and these are then reported on their personal tax returns. This method ensures that earnings are taxed at the individual level, bypassing the issue of double taxation that corporations face. However, it also highlights the necessity for clear, detailed partnership agreements that outline the distribution of profits and losses, ensuring that each partner's tax obligations reflect their share of the venture's financial outcomes.

Tax considerations for partnerships underscore the broader theme of shared financial responsibility and benefit that characterizes these structures. As profits and losses flow directly to the partners, the need for transparency and communication is paramount, not only in terms of operational decisions but also in financial reporting and planning. The partnership agreement, therefore, becomes a critical document, codifying not just the division of profits and losses but also the mechanisms for decision-making, conflict resolution, and, potentially, the dissolution of the partnership. This agreement acts as a roadmap for navigating the complexities of collaboration, ensuring that each partner's contributions and rewards are clearly defined and understood.

In the fabric of partnerships, the threads of collaboration, shared responsibility, and mutual benefit are tightly woven, creating a structure that is both dynamic and delicate. The balance between collective effort and individual risk, between shared decision-making and personal liability, demands not only a legal framework for support but also a foundation of trust and shared vision among the partners. Whether in the equal footing of a general partnership, the hierarchical structure of a limited partnership, or the protective embrace of an LLP, the essence of partnership lies in the synergy of efforts towards a common goal. It is this synergy, carefully nurtured and legally codified, that enables partnerships to thrive as vehicles of collaborative entrepreneurship, harnessing the strengths and aspirations of individuals to create ventures greater than the sum of their parts.

1.4   Corporations: Structure and Scalability

In the pantheon of business structures, corporations stand as titans, characterized by their robust framework designed for expansion and durability. These entities, recognized as independent legal beings, wield the most formidable shield against personal liability for their owners. This delineation between the business and its shareholders ensures that personal assets remain insulated from the corporation's debts and legal obligations, a feature that attracts entrepreneurs aiming to build ventures of significant scale and reach.

Ownership in a corporation is parsed out through shares, a mechanism that democratizes investment and paves the way for a diverse ownership base. This division into shares not only simplifies the process of raising capital by selling equity but also streamlines the transition of ownership, whether it occurs through sales, inheritances, or gifts. The fluidity with which shares can change hands underpins the dynamic nature of corporations, allowing them to adapt to new investors and growth opportunities with relative ease compared to other business structures.

However, the independence and scalability of corporations come at the cost of stringent regulatory compliance. Corporations are bound by a complex web of laws and regulations that dictate everything from their formation to their day-to-day operations. This regulatory framework includes mandatory annual meetings, detailed record-keeping, and the publication of financial statements, ensuring transparency and accountability to shareholders. Furthermore, corporations are required to maintain a board of directors, elected by the shareholders to oversee the major policy and decision-making processes. This layer of governance, while adding a level of procedural complexity, serves as a critical mechanism for aligning the corporation's operations with the shareholders' interests, ensuring strategic coherence and operational integrity.

Taxation represents another dimension of complexity for corporations, particularly in the context of the potential for double taxation. Profits earned by a corporation are first taxed at the corporate level before being distributed as dividends to shareholders, who then pay taxes on these dividends at their personal income tax rates. This cascade of taxation has prompted many corporations to navigate carefully through the tax code, seeking strategies to mitigate their tax liabilities. These strategies include the retention of earnings within the corporation for reinvestment, rather than distribution as dividends, and the utilization of tax deductions and credits available to corporations. Such maneuvers require a nuanced understanding of tax laws and strategic financial planning, underscoring the need for skilled professionals to manage the corporate treasury functions.

Despite the challenges of regulatory compliance and tax complexity, corporations offer unparalleled advantages in terms of scalability and protection. The ability to raise capital through the sale of shares enables corporations to fuel their expansion, investing in new projects, entering new markets, and acquiring other businesses. This capacity for growth is further supported by the corporation's legal status as an independent entity, which facilitates contractual relationships, property ownership, and legal actions in its name, rather than through its shareholders. This independence is a double-edged sword, necessitating a careful balance between strategic ambition and regulatory adherence, but for those ventures with sights set on widespread impact and significant scale, the corporate structure offers a framework equipped to support lofty aspirations.

The intricate dance between growth and governance in corporations is exemplified by the tech giants that dominate global markets. These behemoths, which began as fledgling startups, have leveraged the corporate structure to amass resources, talent, and market share at an unprecedented scale. Their journeys underline the potential of corporations to serve as vessels for transformative ideas, turning nascent inventions into indispensable facets of modern life. Yet, these success stories also highlight the critical role of governance, as the board of directors and executive management navigate the tumultuous waters of global competition, regulatory scrutiny, and shareholder expectations.

In the world of business structures, corporations represent the pinnacle of ambition, offering a blend of protection, scalability, and structure that accommodates ventures of all sizes and stages. From the nascent startup raising its first round of funding to the multinational conglomerate exploring new frontiers of innovation, the corporate structure provides a robust framework for growth and governance. However, this framework demands a meticulous approach to compliance, taxation, and strategic planning, underscoring the importance of professional expertise in navigating the corporate landscape. For entrepreneurs and investors alike, understanding the nuances of the corporate structure is essential for harnessing its potential to build enduring, impactful ventures.

1.5   S-Corporations: Tax Benefits with Conditions

The landscape of corporate structures is nuanced, presenting various pathways for entities to navigate the complexities of taxation and regulation. Among these, the S-Corporation stands as a distinctive choice, offering a blend of corporate identity with certain tax advantages typically reserved for partnerships or sole proprietorships. This hybrid nature is not without its prerequisites and conditions, which meticulously define its operation and the benefits it bestows.

For a corporation to elect S status, it must first satisfy a series of stringent qualifications set forth by the IRS. These include limitations on the number and type of shareholders, with a cap at 100 shareholders who must be individuals, estates, or certain types of trusts. Moreover, these shareholders must be U.S. citizens or permanent residents, a stipulation that underscores the

S-Corp's domestic orientation. This structure cannot have multiple classes of stock, ensuring uniformity in the distribution of dividends and losses. Once these criteria are met, the corporation may file Form 2553 with the IRS, a procedural step that, while straightforward, marks a significant transition in the entity's tax treatment and operational considerations.

The hallmark of the S-Corp structure is its pass-through taxation feature, a mechanism that allows profits, and by extension, taxes, to bypass the corporate veil and flow directly to the shareholders. This arrangement sidesteps the double taxation commonly associated with C-Corporations, where profits are taxed at both the corporate and shareholder levels. Instead, S-Corp earnings are subject only to individual income taxes, a simplification that can significantly reduce the overall tax burden. However, this benefit is tethered to the condition that profits and losses are allocated in proportion to each shareholder's ownership interest, a requirement that demands meticulous financial tracking and reporting.

Navigating the S-Corp landscape further involves adherence to specific regulations regarding shareholder restrictions. The cap on the number of shareholders not only limits the potential for raising capital but also imposes a framework within which the entity must operate. This constraint can affect the company's growth strategies and investment opportunities, demanding a careful balance between the benefits of pass-through taxation and the limitations on ownership expansion. Additionally, the restriction to one class of stock curtails the entity's flexibility in structuring investment deals, requiring creative approaches to financing that do not contravene the S-Corp's stipulations.

A critical aspect of the S-Corp structure involves the distribution of salaries and dividends to shareholder-employees, a process scrutinized under the watchful eyes of the IRS. The agency mandates that shareholder-employees receive a "reasonable" salary for the work they perform, a determination based on industry standards, roles, and responsibilities. This requirement stems from the potential for entities to classify earnings as dividends, which are not subject to employment taxes, thereby circumventing significant tax obligations. Ensuring compliance involves a delicate balance, where the salaries paid reflect the true value of the shareholder-employees' contributions while optimizing the tax advantages inherent in the S-Corp structure.

The interplay between salary and dividend distributions in S-Corporations not only impacts the entity's tax obligations but also shapes the financial landscapes of the shareholder-employees. Dividends, while not subject to employment taxes, are distributed after the allocation of salaries and are contingent upon the entity's profitability. This arrangement necessitates strategic financial planning, both at the corporate and individual levels, to maximize the benefits of the S-Corp's pass-through taxation while adhering to regulatory requirements. The ability to navigate this terrain effectively can significantly influence the entity's operational efficiency and the financial well-being of its shareholders.

In essence, the S-Corporation represents a strategic choice for businesses seeking the legal protections and permanence of a corporate structure, coupled with the tax efficiencies of pass-through entities. Its unique blend of characteristics demands a comprehensive understanding of its qualifications, benefits, and limitations. Entities considering this structure must weigh the implications of shareholder restrictions and the complexities of salary and dividend distributions against the backdrop of their operational goals and growth strategies. Navigating these waters requires not only a keen grasp of the regulatory landscape but also a strategic approach to financial management, ensuring that the entity leverages the S-Corp's advantages while maintaining compliance and optimizing its tax position.

Chapter 2

Legal Frameworks and Liabilities:

Navigating the Maze In the realm of business, the shield of legality not only defends but also defines the contours of entrepreneurial success. This chapter unfurls the tapestry of legal frameworks and liabilities that cloak each business structure, revealing the intricate patterns that must be navigated with precision and care. The choice of business structure, while pivotal in determining tax implications and operational freedom, also casts a long shadow over the realm of legal responsibilities and asset protection. Herein lies the crux of entrepreneurial strategy: balancing the scales of risk and reward within the legal boundaries that define business entities.

2.1   Navigating Liability in Business Structures

Personal vs. Business Liability

The delineation between personal and business liability serves as the first line of defense against the unforeseen tempests of the business world. Sole proprietorships, with their inherent simplicity, expose owners to a direct overflow of business liabilities into personal assets. This conflation of personal and business realms offers no shield against the storms of debt and legal challenges, leaving personal assets vulnerable. In contrast, LLCs and corporations erect a formidable wall between business operations and personal wealth, safeguarding the personal assets of their owners from business-related liabilities. This distinction, fundamental in its implications, mandates a thorough evaluation of the risk landscape inherent in each business structure.

Consider the scenario of a small bookstore facing a lawsuit for copyright infringement. In a sole proprietorship, the owner's personal savings and property might be at risk to settle legal claims. However, had the bookstore been established as an LLC or a corporation, the owner's personal assets would remain insulated from the lawsuit, confined to the realm of business liabilities.

Legal Actions and Consequences

The susceptibility to lawsuits and debts varies significantly across business structures, influenced by the depth of legal separation between the business entity and its owners. Sole proprietorships and partnerships, lacking this separation, find themselves in the direct line of fire, where legal actions against the business directly impinge upon the owners. LLCs and corporations, by virtue of their distinct legal identities, offer their owners a sanctuary, limiting the reach of legal actions to the assets of the business itself. This protective barrier, however, is contingent upon adherence to legal formalities and the maintenance of a clear demarcation between personal and business finances.

2.2   Asset Protection Strategies

Strategies for asset protection transcend the choice of business structure, delving into the realm of strategic financial planning and legal foresight. The utilization of trusts, insurance policies, and separate legal entities for different business ventures or assets can fortify the defense against potential liabilities. Moreover, proactive measures, such as regular legal audits and the establishment of emergency funds, can preemptively address vulnerabilities, ensuring the business remains resilient in the face of legal challenges.

Legal Documentation and Compliance

At the heart of navigating the legal landscape lies the meticulous documentation and unwavering compliance with regulatory requirements. Operating agreements, bylaws, and shareholder agreements emerge as the sinews that bind the entity, delineating roles, responsibilities, and protocols. These documents, coupled with rigorous adherence to state and federal regulations, serve as both shield and compass, guiding the business through the legal complexities of its chosen structure.

Interactive Element: **Business Structure Compliance Checklist**

- **Establish Operating Agreement or Bylaws**: Ensure these foundational documents are in place and fully executed.
- **Annual Reports and Filings:** Mark deadlines on your calendar for state and federal filings to maintain good standing.
- **Separation of Personal and Business Finances:** Regularly review financial practices to ensure a clear demarcation.
- **Legal Audits**: Schedule an annual review with a legal professional to identify and address potential vulnerabilities.

This checklist offers a starting point for entrepreneurs to fortify their ventures against the legal perils that accompany business operations. Adherence to these steps, tailored to the nuances of the chosen business structure, paves the path toward legal resilience and operational stability.

In dissecting the legal frameworks and liabilities associated with each business structure, the entrepreneur is equipped not merely with knowledge but with the power to strategically navigate the complexities of business law. This chapter, while a guide, also serves as a testament to the importance of legal foresight in the architectural design of a business, ensuring that the structure chosen not only supports but also protects the entrepreneurial vision.

2.3   Understanding Tax Obligations for Each Structure

In the labyrinth of entrepreneurship, the specter of taxation looms large, its intricate pathways delineated by the legal form one's business assumes. This section dissects the variegated landscape of tax obligations, revealing the nuanced interplay between business structures and their fiscal responsibilities to federal and state coffers. The endeavor to align one's business with the most advantageous tax framework is not merely an exercise in financial optimization but a strategic imperative that underpins the fiscal health and viability of the enterprise.

Federal Tax Requirements The tax obligations at the federal level present a kaleidoscope of considerations, each hue reflecting the distinctive characteristics of business entities. Sole proprietorships, with their seamless blend of personal and business identities, navigate the terrain of income tax through Schedule C, tethering business profits directly to the owner's personal tax returns. This confluence simplifies the tax process but does not shield the entrepreneur from self-employment taxes, a levy that encompasses both Social Security and Medicare contributions.

LLCs, with their chimeric nature, wield the flexibility to traverse the tax landscape either as disregarded entities or, through election, as corporations. This duality permits the LLC to oscillate between pass-through taxation, mirroring the sole proprietorship's direct route, and the corporate tax structure, embracing the bifurcation of taxation at the entity and dividend levels.

The strategic election of corporate taxation under Subchapter S, for those entities meeting the stringent criteria, further refines this tax navigation, allowing income to pass through to shareholders while eschewing the double taxation paradigm.

Corporations, entrenched in their independent legal status, confront the full spectrum of corporate taxation, a regime that taxes profits at the entity level prior to any dividend distributions. This structure, while offering a bulwark against personal liability, ensnares the entity in the potential for double taxation, where profits are taxed first corporately, then individually upon distribution.

The intricacies of employment taxes further embroider the tax obligations of business entities, with corporations and LLCs acting as employers bearing the responsibility for withholding and remitting taxes on behalf of their employees. This duty, encompassing income tax withholding along with Social Security and Medicare contributions, underscores the administrative and financial burdens shouldered by entities within these structures.

State and Local Taxes

The tax landscape, however, extends beyond the federal horizon, dipping into the variegated terrain of state and local taxation. Here, the business structure once again dictates the route, with state income taxes, franchise taxes, and sales taxes weaving a complex web of obligations that vary not only by structure but by geographic location. The LLC, for instance, might negotiate the currents of state-level pass-through taxation in one jurisdiction, only to confront franchise taxes as a cost of existence in another.

This variability mandates a localized lens through which tax obligations are viewed, necessitating guidance attuned to the specific regulations and nuances of the entity's domicile. The pursuit of tax efficiency thus becomes a geographic as well as structural endeavor, requiring a detailed map of state and local tax landscapes to navigate effectively.

Tax Filing Deadlines and Procedures

The temporal dimension of taxation, marked by filing deadlines and procedural mandates, introduces an additional layer of complexity. Sole proprietorships and

LLCs, tethered as they are to personal tax returns, find their deadlines intertwined with the individual filing date of April 15th. Corporations, charting a course through the calendar year, anchor their filing deadline to March 15th, a temporal marker that delineates their fiscal responsibilities.

This calendrical navigation is further complicated by the procedural rituals of tax filing, from the preparation of the requisite forms to the electronic or paper submission of the tax return. The adherence to these deadlines and procedures, punctuated by the potential for extensions and estimated tax payments, constitutes a critical aspect of tax compliance, necessitating meticulous planning and organizational acuity.

Tax Planning Strategies

Amidst the formidable terrain of tax obligations, tax planning emerges as a beacon of strategy, illuminating paths to fiscal efficiency and optimization. For entities navigating the pass-through taxation of sole proprietorships, LLCs, and S-corporations, the strategic allocation of income and deductions can attenuate tax liabilities, leveraging the personal thresholds and rates to the entity's advantage.

Corporations, ensnared in the web of double taxation, might seek refuge in the strategic retention of earnings, deferring dividend distributions to mitigate the immediate tax impact. Conversely, the meticulous structuring of salary and dividend distributions in S-corporations can optimize the balance between salary (subject to employment taxes) and dividends (exempt from such levies), crafting a tax-efficient remuneration strategy.

This strategic tax planning, woven into the fabric of each business structure, demands not only an intimate understanding of the tax code but a visionary approach to financial architecture. It is within this confluence of knowledge and strategy that entities can sculpt their tax obligations, aligning their fiscal responsibilities with their overarching ambitions for growth and sustainability.

Intellectual Property Considerations

In the intricate web of modern business operations, intellectual property (IP) emerges as a pivotal asset, its value often surpassing the tangible. The safeguarding of these intangible assets within the framework of chosen business structures becomes not merely an operational necessity but a strategic imperative. The delineation of ownership and the mechanisms for protection, licensing, and dispute resolution of IP are significantly influenced by the structural foundation upon which a business is built, thereby necessitating a nuanced understanding of the interplay between IP considerations and business entities.

Ownership and Protection

The architecture of business entities dictates the contours within which the ownership and protection of IP are defined and enforced. Sole proprietorships, with their conflation of personal and business identities, grant the proprietor unequivocal ownership of IP assets. However, this unshielded merger exposes IP to personal liability risks, embedding vulnerabilities within the very fabric of ownership. Conversely, LLCs and corporations, by virtue of their distinct legal existence, provide a bulwark of protection around IP assets, severing them from the personal liabilities of their members or shareholders. This separation not only fortifies the IP against external encroachments but also facilitates its transfer and succession, ensuring continuity and stability in the custodianship of intellectual assets.

The establishment of a corporation further elaborates the matrix of IP ownership, allowing for the allocation of IP rights among shareholders through intricate agreements that delineate the parameters of use, distribution, and revenue. This collective ownership model, while complex, offers a robust framework for the exploitation and management of IP, leveraging the corporate entity as a vehicle for the strategic deployment of intellectual assets.

Licensing and Contracts

The valorization of IP within the business ecosystem is significantly augmented through licensing agreements, contracts that unleash the potential of intellectual assets by stipulating the terms of their utilization by third parties. The crafting of these agreements demands precision, ensuring that the rights of the creator or owner are unequivocally protected while permitting the licensed use of the IP. Within LLCs and corporations, the authority to enter into licensing agreements resides with designated members or executives, their decisions tethered to the strategic objectives of the entity and governed by the overarching contractual framework that binds the entity's operations.

The clarity and specificity of these agreements are paramount, delineating the scope of use, the duration of the license, and the financial arrangements for compensation. This contractual clarity not only safeguards the IP from unauthorized use but also structures the revenue flows from licensing, embedding these agreements within the financial architecture of the business.

IP Disputes and Resolution

Disputes over IP, whether arising from allegations of infringement, breaches of licensing agreements, or contests over ownership, manifest as formidable challenges within the business landscape. The resolution of these disputes is heavily contingent upon the business structure, with sole proprietorships facing the dual peril of personal financial liability and the potential loss of IP rights. LLCs and corporations, insulated from personal liability, navigate these disputes with the corporate entity as the defendant, a stance that, while protective of personal assets, engages the full weight of the business in the resolution process.

Strategies for dispute resolution vary, ranging from negotiation and mediation to arbitration and litigation, each pathway demanding a careful assessment of the potential impacts on the business. The utilization of pre-emptive measures, such as thorough IP audits and the establishment of clear IP policies, serves to mitigate the risk of disputes, embedding a proactive stance towards IP protection within the operational protocols of the business.

Patents and Trademarks The realm of patents and trademarks represents a critical domain of IP, offering legal recognition and protection to inventions and brand identifiers. The process of securing these protections, while uniform in its procedural essence, is inflected by the business structure, influencing the ownership rights and the capacity for enforcement. Sole proprietors, directly registering patents or trademarks, tie these rights closely to their personal legal identity, a simplicity that belies the potential complexities of enforcement and transfer. LLCs and corporations, registering these rights under the entity's name, encapsulate them within the legal shield of the business, ensuring that the rights and enforcement mechanisms are vested in the entity itself.

This encapsulation not only streamlines the process of defense against infringement but also facilitates the strategic deployment of patents and trademarks in the business's market positioning and competitive strategy. Additionally, the ability to license these rights, to monetize the IP through strategic agreements, becomes an integral component of the entity's financial strategy, leveraging the legal protections afforded by patents and trademarks to secure revenue streams and market advantage.

In navigating the multifaceted landscape of IP considerations, the strategic integration of IP management within the chosen business structure emerges as a cornerstone of operational strategy, ensuring not only the protection of intellectual assets but their effective utilization in the pursuit of business objectives.

2.4   Regulatory Compliance Across Structures

Navigating the labyrinth of regulatory compliance demands meticulous attention to detail and an adeptness at maneuvering through the intricacies of laws that vary not just by structure but significantly by industry and geography as well. The obligation to adhere to these regulations is not merely a formality but a critical component of business integrity and public trust. This adherence is multifaceted, enveloping a range of activities from environmental protocols to financial disclosures, each dictated by the nuanced requirements of specific sectors and the overarching mandates of legal bodies.

Industry-Specific Regulations

The tapestry of industry-specific regulations is complex, woven with threads of statutory requirements that cater to the unique characteristics and risks inherent to each sector. For instance, the healthcare industry, steeped in concerns for patient privacy and safety, is governed by stringent regulations like HIPAA in the United States, which mandates the protection of patient information. Conversely, the financial sector is bound by an entirely different set of regulations such as the Dodd-Frank Act, designed to promote financial stability and protect consumers from abusive financial services practices. These examples underscore the necessity for businesses to possess a deep understanding of the regulations that govern their specific industry. This understanding ensures not only compliance but also fortifies the business against potential legal and financial repercussions that can arise from regulatory violations.

State and Federal Compliance The dual specter of state and federal compliance casts a wide net over the operations of a business, each layer adding its own set of rules and requirements. At the federal level, businesses might grapple with the mandates of agencies such as the Environmental Protection Agency (EPA) or the Federal Trade Commission (FTC), depending on their operational focus and impact. These agencies enforce regulations that span environmental standards to consumer protection, necessitating a broad spectrum of compliance activities from businesses operating within their jurisdiction.

On the state level, the diversity in regulations can be even more pronounced, with each state wielding the authority to enact laws that cater to its unique economic, environmental, and social landscapes. This can result in a complex mosaic of compliance obligations for businesses that operate across multiple states, each requiring a tailored approach to regulatory adherence. For instance, a business operating both in California and Texas may need to navigate the California Consumer Privacy Act (CCPA) on one hand and Texas's own set of business regulations on the other, each with its own compliance imperatives.

Periodic Reporting and Renewals

The rhythm of business operations is punctuated by the necessities of periodic reporting and renewals, a cycle that ensures ongoing compliance and the maintenance of good standing within the legal and regulatory framework. This cycle encompasses a variety of filings, from annual reports that outline financial health and operational activities to renewals of permits and licenses that authorize the business to continue its operations within specific jurisdictions or industries. The failure to adhere to these periodic requirements can result in penalties, the revocation of operating privileges, and in severe cases, the dissolution of the business entity itself. Thus, the management of these obligations is paramount, requiring a systematic approach to tracking deadlines, preparing necessary documentation, and submitting filings in a timely manner.

Compliance Resources and Assistance

The path to regulatory compliance, while daunting, is not one that businesses must walk alone. A wealth of resources and assistance is available to guide and support businesses in their compliance journey. Government agencies often provide guidelines, toolkits, and direct assistance programs designed to help businesses understand and meet their regulatory obligations. Furthermore, industry associations play a pivotal role, offering resources specific to the regulatory landscape of their sector, including best practices, compliance checklists, and forums for sharing insights and strategies.

Professional services firms specializing in legal and compliance matters offer another layer of support, providing expert advice and services tailored to the specific needs of the business. These firms can assist with everything from the initial assessment of compliance status to the development of comprehensive compliance programs and the management of reporting and renewals. In addition to these external resources, the cultivation of internal compliance expertise is critical. This can involve the establishment of dedicated compliance teams or the integration of compliance responsibilities into existing roles, ensuring that regulatory adherence is woven into the fabric of daily operations.

The realm of regulatory compliance, with its myriad of requirements and challenges, is a dynamic aspect of business operations that demands constant vigilance and adaptability. The successful navigation of this realm is foundational to the sustainability and growth of a business, safeguarding its legal standing and reinforcing its commitment to operational excellence and integrity. In this light, the pursuit of compliance is not merely a legal obligation but a strategic investment in the future of the enterprise.

2.5   Changing Your Business Structure: Legal Steps

Modifying the foundational architecture of a business structure is a maneuver that, while intricate, is driven by a constellation of motivations. Entities may find themselves at crossroads, where expansion or the quest for enhanced legal protection nudges them towards this transformation. Growth, in its multifaceted dimensions, often outpaces the original structural confines, necessitating a scaffold that can support the burgeoning weight of new opportunities and challenges. Similarly, the shield of legal protection, initially deemed sufficient, may require fortification as the business landscape evolves and exposes new vulnerabilities.

Reasons for Change

The impetus for altering a business structure can emerge from the depths of strategic recalibration, where the pursuit of scalability, investor attraction, or tax optimization becomes the beacon guiding this transition. A sole proprietorship, thriving in its simplicity, might reach a juncture where the allure of attracting venture capital becomes irresistible, pushing towards a corporation's structured embrace. Conversely, a corporation, burdened by the yoke of double taxation, might seek refuge in the pass-through taxation benefits of an S-corporation, aligning fiscal strategy with operational efficiency. Each pivot, marked by a strategic inflection point, underscores the dynamic interplay between business goals and structural form.

Legal Procedures and Documentation

The metamorphosis of a business structure is not without its complexities, entailing a series of legal steps that demand precision and foresight. This odyssey begins with a thorough review of the existing structure's operational agreements and bylaws, dissecting them to identify any constraints or provisions that might impede the intended transformation. Subsequent steps often involve the drafting of new operational agreements or articles of incorporation, tailored to the nuances of the chosen structure. Filings with state and federal agencies, a procedural dance that varies with geographical and structural specifics, become the next hurdle, often necessitating amendments to existing registrations or the submission of new formation documents. This legal ballet, while meticulous, ensures the entity emerges on the other side of transformation legally sound and compliant. Tax Implications

The fiscal landscape, inherently entwined with the business structure, undergoes its own transformation in this process. The shift from a sole proprietorship to an LLC or corporation, for instance, introduces the entity to a new paradigm of tax obligations and benefits. The transition might unveil opportunities for tax savings or expose the entity to new liabilities, making it imperative for businesses to engage in thorough tax planning. This planning, often in concert with tax professionals, navigates the intricate tax implications of the transition, ensuring the business not only remains compliant but also leverages fiscal strategies to its advantage. The interplay between state and federal tax laws, with its labyrinthine complexity, demands a strategic approach that aligns the new structure with the overarching financial vision of the entity.

Transition Strategies

Ensuring continuity and minimizing disruption during this structural metamorphosis requires a tapestry of transition strategies, woven with the threads of communication, planning, and stakeholder engagement. Communicating the impending change to all stakeholders, from employees and customers to vendors and partners, becomes paramount, ensuring the ecosystem surrounding the business is prepared for the transition. Internally, the recalibration of operational processes and systems to align with the new structure demands meticulous planning, ensuring that the entity's day-to-day operations continue to run smoothly. Financial systems, in particular, require a keen eye, ensuring that accounting practices, revenue management, and financial reporting are recalibrated to the nuances of the new structure.

In this complex dance of transformation, the entity stands at the precipice of a new era, poised to navigate the changing business landscape with a structure that aligns with its evolved ambitions and strategies. The journey, while marked by legal, fiscal, and operational challenges, paves the path for a future where the business is better equipped to pursue its goals, protect its assets, and maximize its potential.

In closing, the strategic decision to alter a business's structural foundation is a testament to the entity's evolution and adaptability. This chapter has elucidated the multifaceted considerations and steps involved in such a transition, highlighting the importance of strategic planning, legal compliance, and stakeholder engagement. As we pivot towards the next chapter, we carry forward the understanding that a business's structure is not a static entity but a dynamic framework that must evolve in tandem with the business's growth, aspirations, and the ever-changing market landscape.

Chapter 3

Financial Foundations: Shaping Your Business' Future

When a seed is planted in fertile ground, its growth is not just a matter of chance but a result of the nurturing environment it finds itself in. Similarly, the financial seeding of a business - its initial funding and ongoing financial support - determines not only its growth trajectory but its very survival. This chapter delves into the critical aspect of funding, dissecting how the structural makeup of a business influences its access to capital, the types of investors it attracts, and the innovative funding avenues it can traverse.

3.1 Funding Your Business: Structure Impact

Access to Capital

The structure of a business significantly influences its pathway to securing capital. Sole proprietorships and partnerships often find their access to traditional funding sources like bank loans more challenging, not due to a lack of credibility, but because of the inherent risk lenders perceive in these structures. The personal liability associated with sole proprietorships, for instance, can be a double-edged sword; while it demonstrates the owner's skin in the game, it also raises concerns about the business's ability to withstand financial turbulence.

In contrast, corporations, with their clear legal distinction from their owners, present a less risky proposition to lenders. This distinction reassures lenders of a buffer against defaults, making corporations more likely to secure loans. Moreover, the ability of corporations to issue stock is a unique capital-raising feature that opens doors to equity financing options not available to other structures. This ability to tap into a wider pool of resources is akin to a plant having access to both sunlight and rich soil; it's an advantage that can significantly accelerate growth.

Venture Capital and Angel Investors

Venture capital (VC) and angel investors, with their appetite for high-growth potential businesses, show a marked preference for structured and scalable entities like corporations, particularly those with a C or S designation. This preference stems from the investment-friendly nature of corporations, which allows for an equity exchange without entangling personal assets. The allure of potential high returns on investment makes corporations with innovative products or services particularly attractive to these investors. It's a symbiotic relationship; just as a gardener selects the most promising seeds to cultivate, venture capitalists and angel investors seek out businesses with the structure in place to grow rapidly and deliver substantial returns.

Loans and Credit

The journey to secure loans and credit lines is often a reflection of a business's structural integrity and perceived stability. Banks and credit institutions conduct thorough due diligence, assessing not only the business plan and market potential but also the legal structure as a measure of risk. For LLCs and corporations, the ability to provide collateral separate from personal assets can facilitate the approval process for loans and lines of credit. This separation acts as a safeguard, ensuring that personal financial health is not directly tied to the business's borrowing actions. It's a protective gear for entrepreneurs, akin to wearing a life jacket when navigating the unpredictable currents of business financing

Crowdfunding and Alternative Funding

Crowdfunding represents a modern-day agora, a public square where businesses can present their ideas and garner financial support from a broad audience. This method of funding has democratized access to capital, allowing businesses of all sizes and structures to pitch directly to potential backers. The success of a crowdfunding campaign often hinges on the compelling nature of the business idea rather than the formal structure of the entity. However, corporations and LLCs might have an edge in leveraging crowdfunding successfully, thanks to their ability to offer equity or profit-sharing as part of their fundraising appeal. This approach can be particularly appealing in platforms that cater to equity crowdfunding, where contributors become vested in the business's success.

Interactive Element: **Funding Strategy Assessment**

A reflective exercise designed to help entrepreneurs evaluate their current funding strategies and explore new avenues. This assessment prompts critical thinking about the alignment between the business structure and its financing needs, encouraging a proactive approach to securing the financial foundation necessary for growth.

1. **Current Structure Analysis:** Assess how your current business structure impacts your access to traditional financing options. Are there limitations you need to address?
2. **Investor Attractiveness:** Consider whether your business structure is appealing to the types of investors you aim to attract. What changes, if any, could make your business more attractive to these investors?
3. **Alternative Funding Viability**: Reflect on the suitability of alternative funding methods, such as crowdfunding, for your business. How does your business structure influence this suitability?
4. **Strategic Funding Plan:** Based on your analysis, outline a strategic funding plan that considers both short-term needs and long-term growth objectives. How will you balance the pursuit of loans, investor capital, and alternative funding sources?

This assessment, while a simple exercise, encourages a deep dive into the strategic planning necessary for securing a business's financial future. It underscores the importance of not just understanding but actively managing the interplay between business structure and funding strategies, ensuring that the business is positioned to thrive in an ever-evolving financial landscape.

3.2   Profit Distribution in Different Structures

The allocation of profits within a business structure

operates as the lifeblood of financial reward for the efforts and risks undertaken by entrepreneurs and investors alike. This section explores the nuanced mechanisms through which profits flow from the business entity to the stakeholders, dissected through the lens of various business structures, each with its distinct fiscal and operational DNA. Direct Profit Allocation

In the realm of sole proprietorships and partnerships, the distribution of profits is a direct and unmediated process, reflecting the intimate link between the business's financial performance and the personal income of its owners. In a sole proprietorship, profits generated from the business activities seamlessly transition into the personal earnings of the owner, subject to personal income tax. This direct allocation mechanism underscores the simplicity and personal nature of the structure, where the business essentially functions as an extension of the proprietor's financial persona.

Partnerships, while embodying a collaborative structure, adhere to a similar principle of direct profit allocation. However, the process embraces a layer of complexity, as profits must be divided among partners according to predetermined ratios outlined in the partnership agreement. This division, while straightforward in theory, requires meticulous accounting and transparency to ensure that each partner receives their equitable share of the profits, reflective of their contribution and stake in the business venture.

Dividends and Distributions

The architecture of profit distribution within corporations introduces the concept of dividends, a mechanism that delineates the separation between the entity and its owners. Corporations, by their discrete legal identity, accumulate profits independently of their shareholders, leading to a decision point: to retain earnings within the company or distribute them as dividends. Dividend distributions are determined by the board of directors and represent a portion of the profits returned to shareholders, proportional to their shareholdings. This method of profit distribution, while offering a structured approach to reward investment, also introduces a temporal delay and a layer of decision-making that distances shareholders from the immediate fruits of the company's financial performance.

Limited Liability Companies (LLCs) enjoy a position of flexibility in the distribution of profits, a trait that allows them to adapt profit-sharing mechanisms to the specific needs and goals of the members. Unlike the fixed nature of dividend distributions in corporations, LLCs can allocate profits in a manner that may not necessarily align with ownership percentages, providing a tailored approach to financial rewards. This flexibility, however, requires a solid foundational agreement among members to prevent disputes and ensure clarity in the distribution process.

Tax Implications of Profit Distribution

The tax treatment of profit distributions further complicates the landscape, introducing significant considerations that influence the choice of business structure and distribution strategy. Sole proprietorships and partnerships, with their pass-through taxation, ensure that profits are taxed only once, at the individual level.

This direct taxation mechanism, while simplifying the tax process, ties the financial fate of the business directly to the tax obligations of its owners, making personal tax planning an integral part of business financial management. Corporations encounter the challenge of double taxation, where profits are taxed at the corporate level and again as dividends at the shareholder level. This dual imposition necessitates strategic planning to minimize tax liabilities, often leading corporations to retain earnings rather than distribute them. S-Corporations, with their election to pass through taxation, mitigate this challenge, allowing profits to flow directly to shareholders without the intermediary step of corporate taxation, thus avoiding the double taxation pitfall.

Retained Earnings and Reinvestment

The decision to retain earnings rather than distribute them as dividends or direct profits encapsulates a strategic pivot towards reinvestment and long-term growth. Corporations, in particular, are positioned to leverage retained earnings as a reservoir of capital for reinvestment in operational expansion, research and development, or debt reduction. This strategic reinvestment serves as a catalyst for future profitability, creating a cycle of growth that benefits the company and, by extension, its shareholders. The calculation to retain earnings, however, is a delicate balance, weighing the immediate financial desires of shareholders against the long-term growth potential of the company.

LLCs, while not bound by the same formalities as corporations, also navigate the terrain of retained earnings and reinvestment. The flexibility inherent in the LLC structure allows for a dynamic approach to profit allocation, enabling the entity to channel funds towards growth initiatives as agreed upon by the members. This adaptability ensures that LLCs can respond swiftly to opportunities for expansion or innovation, harnessing retained earnings as a tool for strategic development.

In dissecting the mechanisms of profit distribution across different business structures, it becomes evident that the path from business earnings to stakeholder reward is a journey marked by strategic decisions, tax considerations, and the overarching goals of the entity and its members. The choice of structure, far from being a mere legal formality, plays a pivotal role in shaping the financial landscape of the business, influencing not only how profits are allocated but also how they are leveraged for growth and sustainability. This exploration of profit distribution mechanisms underscores the intricate dance between financial management and strategic planning, a dance that defines the rhythm of business success in the diverse ecosystem of entrepreneurial ventures.

3.3   Managing Financial Risk with the Right Structure

In the intricate dance of entrepreneurship, the ability to navigate financial risks with acumen and foresight stands as a testament to a business's resilience and strategic depth. The architecture of a business, foundational in its essence, not only shapes its operational ethos but also its capacity to withstand and maneuver through the financial uncertainties that litter the landscape of commerce. This section delineates a nuanced framework for assessing and managing financial risks, tailored to the distinctive characteristics of various business structures, and underscores the pivotal role of insurance, financial planning, and debt management as instruments of fiscal prudence. Risk Assessment and Management

The assessment of financial risks begins with a meticulous analysis of the external environment, identifying potential threats that could undermine the financial stability of the business. This analysis, however, requires a lens calibrated to the business's structural makeup, recognizing that the inherent risks and their impacts vary significantly across different entities. For instance, a sole proprietorship, with its unshielded exposure to personal liability, faces a unique set of financial risks, primarily revolving around the potential for personal asset forfeiture in the event of business failure or legal entanglements. Conversely, corporations and LLCs, cloaked in the protection of their separate legal identities, grapple with risks tied to regulatory compliance, shareholder expectations, and the complexities of corporate governance.

The management of these identified risks necessitates a strategic approach, integrating risk mitigation techniques such as diversification of revenue streams, legal safeguards against liability, and the cultivation of a robust compliance culture. For corporations, this might entail the implementation of stringent governance protocols and the establishment of compliance departments, whereas sole proprietorships may focus on personal asset protection strategies and operational risk diversification. This tailored approach to risk management not only fortifies the business against the vicissitudes of the financial landscape but also aligns risk mitigation efforts with the structural realities of the entity.

Insurance and Protection Strategies

In the arsenal of risk management tools, insurance emerges as a critical ally, offering a bulwark against the financial fallout of unforeseen events. The deployment of insurance, however, is not a one-size-fits-all strategy but one that demands customization to the business structure's unique vulnerabilities. Sole proprietors, for instance, may prioritize personal liability insurance to shield personal assets from business-related claims, a concern less pronounced for corporations and LLCs, where the focus shifts to professional liability and directors' and officers' insurance to protect against claims tied to management decisions.

The strategic selection of insurance policies, from property and casualty to worker's compensation and business interruption insurance, forms a multi-layered defense mechanism, safeguarding the business's financial health against a spectrum of threats. This protective strategy, while representing an upfront cost, is an investment in the business's longevity, providing a safety net that enables the entity to weather storms and emerge with its financial foundations intact.

Financial Planning and Reserves

Central to the ethos of financial risk management is the art of financial planning, a process that extends beyond mere budgeting to encompass the strategic allocation of resources in anticipation of future needs and challenges. This planning process, informed by the business structure, enables entities to forecast financial flows, assess capital requirements, and identify potential funding gaps. For LLCs and corporations, this might involve sophisticated financial modeling to support growth initiatives or capital raises, whereas sole proprietorships may focus on liquidity planning to ensure the owner's personal financial obligations are met.

Integral to effective financial planning is the establishment of financial reserves, a pool of funds earmarked to address unexpected challenges or opportunities. These reserves act as a financial buffer, ensuring the business can navigate short-term disruptions without compromising its long-term strategic objectives. The size and management of these reserves are influenced by the business structure, with corporations perhaps adopting formal reserve policies set by the board, while sole proprietors and partnerships might opt for more fluid approaches to reserve funding.

Debt Management

The prudent management of debt and liabilities stands as a cornerstone of financial stability, ensuring that the business's leverage does not become a straitjacket that constrains growth or jeopardizes fiscal health. Effective debt management strategies are predicated on the understanding that the implications of debt vary across business structures, influencing not only the entity's risk profile but also its operational flexibility. Corporations, with their access to diversified financing options, may employ sophisticated debt instruments, balancing cost and flexibility to optimize their capital structure. Sole proprietorships and partnerships, navigating the delicate interplay between business and personal finances, might prioritize debt strategies that minimize personal liability exposure and protect personal assets.

The calibration of debt levels, the negotiation of terms, and the strategic timing of debt issuance or retirement are critical components of a comprehensive debt management strategy. This strategy, aligned with the entity's financial goals and risk tolerance, ensures that leverage is not merely a means of financing but a strategic tool that enhances the business's capacity to invest, grow, and thrive in the competitive marketplace.

In threading through the multifaceted landscape of financial risk management, the symbiosis between business structure and financial strategy becomes palpably clear. The architecture of the entity not only frames its operational narrative but also its ability to engage with the financial imperatives of risk assessment, insurance, planning, and debt management. This interplay between structure and strategy, intricate in its complexity, is instrumental in crafting a financial blueprint that supports the business's aspirations, ensuring it stands resilient amidst the uncertainties of the economic terrain.

3.4   Tax Strategies for Each Business Structure

The labyrinth of taxation presents a formidable challenge across the diverse spectrum of business structures. Here, the astute manipulation of tax-related variables becomes a pivotal driver of fiscal efficiency. Delving into the realm of tax strategies, a nuanced exploration reveals the tailored approaches businesses can employ, each structure offering unique pathways to mitigate tax liabilities while bolstering financial health.

Maximizing Deductions

For entities structured as sole proprietorships, the direct blending of business and personal finances provides a fertile ground for tax deductions. Expenses that straddle the line between personal and business use, such as home office deductions or the use of a personal vehicle for business, demand meticulous documentation and judicious apportionment. This careful delineation ensures the maximization of deductible expenses, directly reducing taxable income.

Partnerships, engaging in operations where expenses are jointly incurred, find their strength in pooling deductions. The strategic allocation of expenses across partners, in alignment with partnership agreements, can optimize deductible outcomes, provided the expenses are squarely for business purposes. This shared approach extends to the deduction of losses, where partners can offset personal income with their share of the business's losses, a tactic that demands precise calculation to align with individual tax situations.

Corporations, navigating the intricate waters of corporate tax, employ deductions as a lever to lower their taxable income. Strategies here include the aggressive depreciation of assets through accelerated depreciation methods and the deduction of employee benefit programs, which not only reduce taxable income but also enhance the company's value proposition to its workforce. The careful orchestration of these deductions requires a deep understanding of tax law nuances, ensuring that the corporation remains within the bounds of legality while maximizing its tax benefits.

LLCs, with their chameleon-like tax status, adapt their deduction strategies based on their elected tax treatment. Those opting for corporation tax status might mirror corporate strategies, while those under pass-through taxation align more closely with sole proprietorship or partnership methodologies. The flexibility inherent in the LLC structure allows for a dynamic approach to deductions, one that can be recalibrated in response to changes in the business environment or tax legislation.

Employment Tax Considerations

Sole proprietorships confront employment taxes head-on, with the business owner responsible for both the employee and employer portions of Social Security and Medicare taxes, a substantial burden that underscores the importance of strategic tax planning to mitigate its impact.

Partnerships face a similar scenario, where partners acting in roles that contribute labor to the business are subject to self-employment taxes on their distributive share. The delineation of active versus passive partners becomes crucial here, as passive partners may be exempt from these taxes, providing a strategic framework for structuring participation in the business to optimize tax outcomes.

Corporations introduce a layer of separation in employment taxes, with the entity itself assuming the employer's portion of these taxes. This separation provides a buffer for shareholders from direct employment tax liabilities but necessitates rigorous payroll management to ensure compliance and optimization of tax obligations.

Capital Gains Strategies

For corporations, particularly C-corporations, capital gains present both a challenge and an opportunity. The corporate structure subjects capital gains to double taxation, first at the corporate level and again at the shareholder level upon distribution. Strategic timing of asset sales and the use of capital losses to offset gains become critical maneuvers to mitigate the impact of capital gains taxes. Additionally, corporations might explore structuring certain transactions to qualify for installment sales, spreading capital gains recognition over several years to manage tax liabilities more effectively.

LLCs enjoy a more direct pathway in managing capital gains, with the ability to pass through these gains to members, who then report them on their personal tax returns. This pass-through mechanism allows for individual members to apply personal capital losses against gains, offering a nuanced strategy to manage capital gains tax liabilities. The flexibility of the LLC structure in managing distributions provides an additional layer of strategy in timing and allocating gains to optimize tax outcomes.

Retirement and Benefit Planning

Retirement and benefit planning within sole proprietorships and partnerships integrates closely with personal financial planning, offering a streamlined approach to retirement savings.

Simplified Employee Pension (SEP) plans and solo 401(k)s are potent tools in this domain, allowing for significant tax-deferred contributions that not only lower current taxable income but also build a foundation for future financial security.

Corporations, leveraging their entity status, can establish comprehensive retirement and benefit plans, including traditional 401(k)s and defined benefit plans. These plans not only serve as a deductible expense for the corporation, reducing taxable income, but also enhance the corporate value proposition, aiding in the attraction and retention of top talent. The strategic deployment of these plans requires a careful balance between fiscal impact and operational goals, ensuring that the benefits offered align with the company's long-term strategic objectives and financial health.

The LLC, with its adaptable structure, can mirror the strategies applicable to sole proprietorships, partnerships, or corporations, based on its chosen tax treatment. This adaptability provides LLCs with a broad palette of options in retirement and benefit planning, allowing them to tailor their strategies to best meet the needs of their members and the operational goals of the business.

In navigating the dense forest of tax strategies, entities across the spectrum of business structures find unique pathways to mitigate liabilities and optimize financial outcomes. The careful calibration of these strategies, tailored to the legal and operational framework of the business, becomes a critical component of financial management, ensuring that the entity not only survives but thrives in the competitive marketplace.

3.5 Planning for Financial Growth

Financial growth, a beacon for any business, requires more than just ambition; it necessitates meticulous planning and a strategic approach tailored to the unique fabric of each business structure. This planning goes beyond mere aspiration, embedding itself in the operational and structural DNA of the entity, guiding its trajectory from nascent venture to thriving enterprise.

Growth Projections and Planning

The foresight to project financial growth is akin to charting a course through uncharted waters, relying on a combination of historical data, market analysis, and predictive modeling. For sole proprietorships, this process is deeply personal, blending the owner's financial destiny with that of the business. Projections must account for personal financial commitments and the business's operational needs, a balancing act that requires a keen understanding of cash flow dynamics and market opportunities.

LLCs and corporations, with their distinct legal identities, approach growth projections with a broader lens, incorporating not only operational data but also market position and competitive analysis. These entities often leverage sophisticated financial models that simulate various scenarios, from expansion into new markets to the introduction of new product lines. This approach allows for a dynamic planning process, where strategies can be adjusted in response to changing market conditions or internal performance metrics.

For partnerships, the collaborative nature of the structure informs the planning process, necessitating alignment among partners on growth objectives and strategies. This alignment ensures that projections reflect a shared vision, incorporating the diverse expertise and perspectives of the partners to create a multifaceted growth strategy that leverages the collective strengths of the entity.

Reinvesting Profits for Growth

The reinvestment of profits stands as a testament to a business's commitment to its future, channeling today's financial successes into tomorrow's growth opportunities. Sole proprietorships face the challenge of distinguishing between personal and business finances in this process, often requiring disciplined financial management to ensure that sufficient profits are reinvested to support business objectives.

In contrast, LLCs and corporations possess the structural capacity to delineate profit reinvestment more clearly, establishing formal mechanisms for the allocation of profits to strategic growth initiatives. This may include investing in research and development, expanding operational capacity, or pursuing acquisitions to bolster market position. The decision-making process around reinvestment is strategic, informed by a comprehensive analysis of return on investment and alignment with long-term strategic goals.

Partnerships, navigating the collective will of the

partners, must forge consensus on reinvestment strategies, ensuring that the allocation of profits for growth reflects the shared objectives of the partners. This consensus-building process is crucial, as it not only determines the direction of growth initiatives but also reinforces the partnership's unity and shared commitment to the business's success.

Financial Metrics and Performance Indicators

The compass guiding a business through its growth journey is the strategic use of financial metrics and performance indicators, tools that provide insight into the health and trajectory of the entity. For sole proprietorships, key metrics may include cash flow analysis, profitability ratios, and debt-to-equity ratios, offering a snapshot of financial stability and operational efficiency.

LLCs and corporations, with their more complex operational structures, employ a broader array of metrics, from return on equity (ROE) and return on investment (ROI) to earnings before interest, taxes, depreciation, and amortization (EBITDA). These metrics offer a granular view of financial performance, informing strategic decisions from investment in new technologies to market expansion strategies.

For partnerships, the focus on performance indicators extends to metrics that reflect the collaborative nature of the entity, including partner contributions and the allocation of profits and losses. These indicators not only measure financial performance but also ensure transparency and equity among partners, reinforcing the trust and mutual commitment that underpin the partnership.

Scaling Operations and Financial Systems

The scaling of operations and financial systems is a critical aspect of supporting sustained growth, requiring an adaptive approach that anticipates the evolving needs of the business. Sole proprietorships, often limited by the capacity of the individual owner, must adopt scalable financial systems early, leveraging technology to automate financial processes and ensure efficient management of increased transaction volumes.

LLCs and corporations face the challenge of scaling operations in a way that maintains the agility of the business while ensuring robust financial controls. This may involve the implementation of enterprise resource planning (ERP) systems, the expansion of financial teams, and the development of scalable processes that can accommodate growth without sacrificing operational efficiency or financial integrity.

For partnerships, the scaling of operations must be approached with an eye towards maintaining alignment among partners, ensuring that the expansion of the business does not dilute the collaborative ethos of the entity. This requires transparent communication, shared decision-making, and the adoption of financial systems that support the collective management of the business.

In navigating the path to financial growth, businesses of all structures must embrace strategic planning, disciplined reinvestment, and the judicious use of financial metrics and scalable systems. This approach not only supports the operational expansion of the entity but also ensures that growth is sustainable, rooted in sound financial management and strategic foresight.

As we transition from the exploration of financial growth strategies, we reflect on the critical importance of aligning these strategies with the structural and operational realities of the business. The journey ahead, while challenging, is rich with opportunities for those prepared to navigate the complexities of financial growth with strategic acumen and a commitment to long-term success.

Chapter 4

Strategic Architecture: Tailoring Structure to Vision

In the tapestry of business, each thread — the decisions, the strategies, the structures — interweaves to create a picture of success or a cautionary tale. The choice of a business structure does not merely lay the groundwork; it shapes the very contours of a venture's future, influencing its growth, agility, and the nature of its interactions within the market ecosystem. This chapter delves into the symbiotic relationship between a business's strategic goals and its structural form, exploring how this alignment acts as a catalyst for sustainable growth and competitive positioning.

4.1 Aligning Business Structure with Strategic Goals

Long-Term Vision and Structure Selection

A business's long-term vision serves as the North Star, guiding strategic decisions including the choice of structure. This vision, encompassing goals for growth, market presence, and operational scale, demands a structural foundation that not only supports but amplifies these objectives. A sole proprietorship, while offering simplicity and direct control, may falter under the weight of ambitious growth targets, lacking the capacity to attract investment or distribute risk.

Conversely, the formal scaffolding of a corporation, designed for scalability and investment attraction, may prove cumbersome for ventures whose vision prioritizes agility and personal control over rapid expansion. This alignment between vision and structure is not static; it requires periodic reassessment to ensure the foundation remains conducive to the venture's evolving aspirations.

Consider a tech startup with aspirations to disrupt the market. The initial choice of an LLC offers flexibility and protection, yet as the startup's vision expands to include public investment and global reach, a transition to a C-corporation might align more closely with these goals, facilitating equity sharing and opening doors to public markets.

Flexibility and Adaptability

In a landscape marked by volatility and rapid evolution, the capacity for flexibility and adaptability becomes a critical determinant of success. Business structures vary widely in their intrinsic ability to accommodate change, from the fluid dynamics of partnerships to the rigid hierarchies of corporations. The strategic selection or modification of a business structure to enhance adaptability can serve as a bulwark against uncertainty, enabling the venture to pivot in response to market demands, regulatory changes, or internal growth challenges. This flexibility extends to operational practices, partnership opportunities, and the exploration of new market segments, ensuring that the venture remains resilient in the face of change.

Strategic Partnerships and Alliances

Strategic partnerships and alliances often serve as key accelerants for growth, providing access to new markets, technologies, and expertise. The choice of business structure can significantly impact a venture's capacity to engage in and benefit from such partnerships. Corporations, with their clear delineation of ownership and governance, may facilitate straightforward equity-based alliances, while the personal nature of sole proprietorships and partnerships may hinder or complicate such arrangements. A venture's structural form must anticipate the potential for strategic alliances, ensuring that the entity is positioned to capitalize on collaborative opportunities without sacrificing control or diluting ownership.

A real-world example is a small software development firm structured as an LLC contemplating an alliance with a larger distributor. The LLC structure allows for a flexible negotiation of terms, potentially enabling profit sharing without equity dilution, a scenario that might prove more complex under a corporate structure.

Market Positioning and Competitive Advantage

The market positioning and competitive advantage of a venture are inextricably linked to its structural form. A business structure influences not only the venture's operational agility and growth potential but also its brand perception and stakeholder relationships. For startups aiming to carve out a niche in crowded markets, the lean operational model of an LLC may convey innovation and agility, while established ventures seeking to assert dominance may find the authoritative presence of a corporation more in line with their market positioning strategy. The strategic alignment of structure with competitive positioning ensures that the venture's foundational architecture supports its market aspirations, enhancing its visibility and appeal to both customers and investors.

Interactive Element: **Strategic Alignment Assessment**

A guided assessment designed to help entrepreneurs evaluate the alignment between their current business structure and their strategic goals. This exercise prompts reflection on long-term vision, flexibility needs, partnership potential, and competitive positioning, offering insights into whether the current structure facilitates or hinders the realization of these objectives.

1. **Vision Alignment**: Reflect on your long-term business goals. Does your current structure provide the necessary support and opportunities to achieve these goals?
2. **Flexibility and Adaptability:** Assess your venture's ability to navigate change. Does your structure allow for quick pivots and adjustments in response to market dynamics?
3. **Partnership Potential**: Consider your goals for strategic alliances. Is your current structure conducive to forming and benefiting from partnerships?
4. **Competitive Positioning:** Evaluate your market positioning strategy. Does your business structure enhance your competitive advantage and brand perception?

This assessment, through a series of targeted questions and scenarios, encourages entrepreneurs to critically analyze the foundation of their ventures, ensuring that the chosen structure not only supports but actively propels them toward their strategic goals.

4.2   The Role of Business Structures in Scaling Operations

Scaling operations, a pivotal aspect of a business's growth trajectory, necessitates an architectural blueprint that not only supports expansion but also optimizes it. The structural DNA of a business plays a critical role in this respect, acting as both a facilitator and a constraint on the path to scalability. The dynamic interplay between a business's structural form and its scaling ambitions calls for a nuanced understanding of how different frameworks can either propel or hinder growth.

Scalability and Structure

The scalability potential inherent in each business structure varies significantly, with corporate forms typically positioned at the vanguard of supporting expansive growth. This is not accidental but by design, as corporations are equipped with mechanisms — such as the ability to issue stock and attract investment — that are indispensable for scaling. These mechanisms not only provide the capital infusion necessary for expansion but also establish a governance framework that can accommodate growth without succumbing to operational chaos. In contrast, the intrinsic simplicity of sole proprietorships, while beneficial in the nascent stages of a venture, often becomes a bottleneck when scaling, as the fusion of personal and business assets limits access to capital and complicates risk distribution. Similarly, partnerships, though more amenable to growth than sole proprietorships, face challenges in aligning the visions and objectives of multiple partners, potentially slowing decision-making processes critical to rapid scaling.

Operational Efficiency and Structure

Operational efficiency, the linchpin of successful scaling, is deeply influenced by the choice of business structure. Corporations, with their delineated roles and hierarchical operational models, are primed for efficiency at scale. This structure facilitates the delegation of responsibilities, streamlining processes, and ensuring that decision-making does not become a bottleneck. However, this efficiency comes with the caveat of potential bureaucratic inertia, a risk that corporations must navigate carefully. LLCs strike a balance, offering a more flexible operational framework that can adapt more readily to the demands of scaling, blending the agility of less formal structures with the protective and organizational advantages of corporate form. This adaptability makes LLCs particularly suited to businesses whose growth trajectories require a nimble operational approach.

Managing Growth Challenges

Growth, while desirable, introduces a spectrum of challenges, from staffing to resource allocation, each magnified by the underlying business structure. For sole proprietorships transitioning into more expansive operations, the challenge often lies in moving beyond personal networks for staffing and embracing formal HR processes, a shift that can strain the informal operational ethos of the structure. LLCs and corporations, designed with growth in mind, face the challenge of maintaining organizational culture and operational coherence amid rapid expansion. This requires a meticulous approach to talent acquisition, training, and integration, ensuring that the human capital scales in tandem with operational needs. Resource allocation, too, becomes a strategic exercise in prioritization, demanding a keen understanding of the venture's core value drivers and the most efficient deployment of capital to fuel growth.

Expansion Considerations

Expansion, whether through geographic diversification or the exploration of new product lines, is a strategic lever for growth that is deeply influenced by business structure. Corporations, with their ability to raise capital through equity and debt, are well-positioned to fund ambitious expansion plans, leveraging their structured governance models to coordinate complex

multi-faceted growth strategies. This capacity for raising and deploying capital efficiently makes corporations particularly adept at pursuing both geographic and product line expansions aggressively. LLCs, while more flexible, must carefully navigate expansion to ensure that the venture remains within the operational and financial bandwidth of its members, often requiring creative approaches to funding and strategic partnerships to achieve growth objectives. For sole proprietorships and partnerships, expansion considerations are tightly interwoven with personal financial risk and the capacity for management oversight, necessitating a cautious approach that balances growth ambitions with the practical constraints of the structure.

In sum, the path to scaling operations is intricately bound to the structural foundations of a business, with each form offering distinct advantages and challenges in the pursuit of growth. The strategic alignment of structure with scaling ambitions is not merely a matter of preference but a critical determinant of success, requiring a deep understanding of the operational, financial, and strategic dimensions of growth. As businesses navigate the complexities of scaling, the choice of structure emerges as a pivotal axis around which expansion strategies revolve, underscoring the importance of structural adaptability, operational efficiency, and strategic foresight in the architecture of growth.

4.3 Pivoting: When and How to Change Your Structure

Indicators for Structural Change

Within the dynamic sphere of business, certain signals underscore the necessity for a structural metamorphosis. These markers often emerge from the depths of operational inefficiencies, legal constraints, or financial stagnation—each a siren call for reevaluation. A palpable sign is the strain on resources that were once ample, now stretched thin by the burgeoning demands of a growing enterprise, indicating that the initial structure no longer accommodates the business's expanded scope. Legal limitations, too, serve as a clarion call, especially when the venture's activities brush against the ceiling of permissible operations under its current legal form, perhaps stifling opportunities for raising capital or entering new markets. Financial indicators, particularly those related to taxation and profit distribution, often reveal inefficiencies that could be ameliorated by a shift in structure, signaling the potential for enhanced fiscal health through a strategic pivot.

Evaluating New Structures

Navigating the transition to a new business structure requires a methodical approach, commencing with a meticulous evaluation of potential forms against the backdrop of current and projected operational, legal, and financial landscapes. This assessment begins with a granular analysis of operational needs, discerning which structure offers the optimal balance of flexibility, control, and scalability to support the business's ambitions. Legal considerations follow, with a focus on liability exposure, regulatory compliance, and the capacity to engage in desired financial transactions, ensuring the chosen structure provides a conducive legal framework for the venture's activities. Financial analysis, too, is paramount, scrutinizing how different structures impact taxation, capital raising, and profit retention, aiming to identify the form that aligns with fiscal efficiency and growth financing strategies. This evaluative process, while intricate, is foundational, laying the groundwork for a structural pivot that aligns with the venture's strategic trajectory.

Implementation Plan for Structure Change

Transitioning to a new business structure unfolds as a sequence of deliberate steps, each meticulously planned to ensure legal compliance, operational continuity, and stakeholder communication. The initiation of this process demands a formal decision, often solidified through resolutions or agreements among the current entity's owners or board members, setting the stage for the transformation. Legal registrations follow, involving the filing of necessary paperwork with relevant state and federal bodies to establish the new entity and dissolve or alter the existing one, a step that often requires legal counsel to navigate complex regulatory waters. Financial adjustments constitute the next phase, entailing modifications to banking arrangements, accounting systems, and tax registrations to reflect the new structure, ensuring fiscal operations proceed without interruption. Throughout this transition, clear and consistent communication with stakeholders, including employees, customers, investors, and suppliers, is pivotal, mitigating concerns and fostering a sense of stability during the change. Minimizing Disruption During Transition

The metamorphosis of a business structure, while strategic, harbors the potential for operational disruption, necessitating strategies to maintain business continuity. One such strategy involves phased implementation, gradually introducing structural changes to allow for adjustment and adaptation within the operational ecosystem, thereby reducing the shock to routine processes and relationships. Parallel operations also emerge as a viable approach, running the old and new structures concurrently for a limited period to ensure a seamless transition of functions and responsibilities, a tactic that provides a safety net should unforeseen challenges arise. Training and support for employees are crucial, equipping the human capital with the knowledge and tools necessary to navigate the new operational landscape effectively, ensuring that the pivot enhances rather than hinders the business's functional capabilities. Lastly, leveraging technology to automate and streamline transition processes can significantly reduce the manual burden on staff, allowing for a focus on core operations and strategic initiatives amidst the structural shift.

In this complex dance of structural evolution, the business stands at a crossroads, with each sign, each evaluation, and each meticulously planned step guiding the way to a form that not only matches its current stride but anticipates its future pace. The decision to pivot, grounded in a deep understanding of the business's operational, legal, and financial fabric, unfolds as a strategic maneuver aimed at unlocking new horizons of growth, efficiency, and market relevance. This transformative journey, while fraught with challenges, is a testament to the business's agility, foresight, and unwavering commitment to its long-term vision, ensuring that the structural form remains not just a vessel but a catalyst for sustained success and innovation.

4.4   Exit Strategies and Business Structure

In the strategic contemplation of business architecture, the integration of exit strategies often emerges as an afterthought, overshadowed by the immediacy of growth and operational efficacy. Yet, the foresight to weave exit mechanisms into the structural blueprint from inception not only accentuates the agility of a business in responding to future market shifts but also maximizes value for its stakeholders in scenarios of dissolution, sale, or succession. This nuanced interplay between the choice of business structure and the articulation of exit pathways underscores the necessity for entrepreneurs to consider the end as much as the beginning in their strategic planning.

Planning for Exit

The contemplation of an exit strategy, an intrinsic part of the strategic horizon, necessitates a discerning eye towards the eventualities that might compel a business to change hands, merge, dissolve, or transition. The inevitability of such transitions, whether driven by personal circumstances, market dynamics, or strategic realignment, demands an anticipatory approach in the selection of a business structure. This approach ensures that the legal and operational framework of the business does not become an impediment to the realization of exit objectives but rather facilitates a smooth transition, preserving or enhancing value in the process. It is this strategic alignment between structure and exit objectives that enables businesses to navigate potential future transitions with grace and precision.

Structure-Specific Exit Options

The lattice of exit options available to a business intricately intertwines with its structural form, each presenting unique pathways and challenges to realization. Sole proprietorships, embodying the unity of ownership and operation, often face a straightforward yet personal exit through sale or closure. However, the personal entanglement of assets and liabilities necessitates meticulous planning to ensure personal financial stability post-exit. Partnerships, with their collective ownership model, introduce complexities in exit scenarios, particularly in buyouts or dissolution, where the equitable distribution of assets and liabilities amongst partners demands a carefully crafted partnership agreement that preempts exit contingencies.

Corporations, with their delineated ownership and operational structure, offer a spectrum of exit strategies, from public offerings, which enable the original stakeholders to liquidate their holdings in the market, to mergers and acquisitions, where the corporate entity can be sold or merged, offering a potentially lucrative exit for shareholders. The clarity and formality of the corporate structure facilitate these transactions, providing a legal and operational framework that supports complex exit scenarios. Limited Liability Companies (LLCs), embodying a hybrid structure, afford flexibility in exit planning, enabling members to tailor exit provisions within the operating agreement to align with their strategic objectives, whether through member buyouts, sale of the company, or other mechanisms.

Valuation and Sale Considerations

The valuation and eventual sale of a business are profoundly influenced by its structural composition, impacting both the methodology of valuation and the attractiveness of the business to potential buyers. In sole proprietorships and partnerships, the valuation often hinges on the personal reputation and client relationships developed by the owners, posing a challenge in quantifying and transferring this intangible value to new owners. This personal dependency can impact the sale price and attractiveness to buyers, necessitating strategic initiatives to institutionalize business operations and client relationships.

Corporations and LLCs, benefiting from a separation between personal and business operations, often enjoy a clearer pathway to valuation, with established financial metrics and market comparables providing a basis for assessment. This clarity enhances the business's marketability to a broader spectrum of buyers, from strategic acquirers to financial investors, potentially driving higher valuation multiples. The structural form here not only influences the valuation methodology but also the negotiation dynamics, with formal governance structures providing a framework for transparent and structured sale processes.

Succession Planning

Succession planning, particularly within family-owned businesses and partnerships, encapsulates the strategic foresight to ensure business continuity across generations or changes in partnership. This planning, deeply personal yet critical to the longevity of the business, demands a structural framework that supports the seamless transition of ownership and operational roles. In family-owned enterprises, the choice between maintaining a sole proprietorship and incorporating often hinges on the desire for continuity and the division of ownership among heirs. The incorporation of the business can facilitate this transition, allowing for the distribution of shares and the establishment of governance structures that delineate operational roles and decision-making authority.

Partnerships, navigating the complexities of multiple owners, benefit from the explicit articulation of succession provisions within the partnership agreement, detailing the mechanisms for partner exits, entry of new partners, and the valuation of partnership interests. These provisions not only ensure clarity and fairness in transitions but also preserve the operational integrity and strategic direction of the business, safeguarding its value through periods of change.

In the strategic architecture of a business, the integration of exit strategies into the choice of structure emerges as a critical facet of planning, ensuring that the eventual transition, sale, or succession not only preserves but potentially enhances the value of the business for its stakeholders. This anticipatory approach underscores the importance of strategic depth and foresight in the foundational planning of a venture, ensuring that the business is not only poised for growth and operational efficacy but also prepared for the eventualities of change, transition, and succession.

4.5   Future-proofing Your Business with the Right Structure

In a world where change is the only constant, businesses must adapt or risk obsolescence. The architecture of a business, its structural core, significantly influences its capacity to navigate the waters of change, be it through market shifts, regulatory evolutions, or the imperative for innovation. A well-chosen structure not only supports a business's current operational and strategic needs but also anticipates the winds of change, enabling the entity to adjust its sails swiftly and efficiently.

Anticipating Market Changes

The ability to anticipate and adapt to market changes is a critical determinant of business longevity. Different structures offer varying degrees of agility, influencing how swiftly a business can pivot in response to evolving market dynamics. Sole proprietorships and LLCs, with their streamlined decision-making processes, inherently possess a high degree of adaptability, enabling rapid responses to market fluctuations. However, this agility comes at the cost of the broader resource base and structural support offered by corporate forms, which, despite their more complex decision-making apparatus, benefit from a depth of resources and strategic positioning that can be leveraged to navigate market changes. The challenge lies in striking a balance between agility and stability, choosing a structure that allows for quick adaptation while providing a steady foundation for growth.

Innovation and Structure Innovation, the lifeblood of competitive advantage, thrives in environments that foster creativity and swift implementation. The relationship between business structure and innovation is nuanced, shaped by the structure's capacity to support experimentation, risk-taking, and the dynamic allocation of resources. Corporations, particularly those with strategic divisions dedicated to research and development, can marshal significant resources towards innovation efforts. However, the bureaucratic layers often present in corporate environments can dampen the entrepreneurial spirit, potentially slowing the pace of innovation. In contrast, the lean operational models of sole proprietorships and LLCs often create fertile ground for innovation, where ideas can be tested and implemented without the encumbrance of extensive procedural hurdles. The key lies in crafting a structure that encapsulates the best of both worlds—resource availability and operational agility—creating an ecosystem where innovation can flourish.

Regulatory Landscape and Future Trends

The regulatory landscape, ever-evolving in response to societal, economic, and technological trends, exerts a profound influence on the operational terrain of businesses. Anticipating regulatory changes and understanding their potential impact on different business structures is essential for future-proofing a venture. For instance, emerging trends in digital privacy laws may impact LLCs and corporations differently, depending on their customer engagement models and data handling practices. Similarly, changes in international trade regulations can have varied implications for businesses depending on their structure and market exposure. Staying abreast of these changes and building a flexible, informed compliance strategy into the business structure can mitigate risks and leverage regulatory shifts as opportunities for innovation and market differentiation.

Building a Resilient Business Model

At the core of future-proofing lies the construction of a resilient business model, one that withstands economic fluctuations and market shifts while maintaining the flexibility to adapt and grow. This resilience is intrinsically linked to the choice of business structure, which dictates the venture's operational flexibility, funding mechanisms, and capacity for innovation. A resilient model is not static; it evolves, incorporating lessons from past challenges and insights into future trends, continuously refining its structural and operational underpinnings. The incorporation of digital technologies, diversification of revenue streams, and cultivation of a robust organizational culture are pillars upon which this resilience is built, each supported by a business structure that aligns with the venture's strategic vision and operational realities.

In navigating the complexities of future-proofing a business, the interplay between structure, market anticipation, innovation capacity, regulatory adaptability, and resilience construction becomes evident. Each element, while distinct, is interconnected, forming a cohesive strategy that not only safeguards the business against the unpredictability of the future but also positions it to seize emerging opportunities. The choice of structure, far from being a mere formality, is a strategic decision that underpins the venture's capacity to thrive amidst change, embodying the principles of adaptability, foresight, and strategic alignment. As we move forward, it's clear that the architecture of a business, its structural foundation, holds the keys to not just surviving but thriving in a landscape marked by continuous change. The insights gleaned from this exploration underscore the importance of strategic alignment, adaptability, and resilience in crafting a business model that stands the test of time, ready to face the challenges and opportunities that lie ahead.

Review Page

"Mastering Business Structures"

"Your guide to choosing the right structure for your business, legal frameworks, profit maximizing, and growth securing"

Dear Esteemed Reader,

We hope this message finds you well. DA Affiliates 2, is committed to providing valuable resources to empower entrepreneurs and business leaders on their journey to success. We are thrilled to announce the release of our latest publication, "Mastering Business Structures", a comprehensive guide designed to equip you with the knowledge and tools needed to navigate the complex world of business structures effectively.

Why Your Feedback Matters

Your feedback is invaluable to us as we strive to continuously improve and tailor our content to meet your needs and expectations. By sharing your thoughts and insights on "Mastering Business Structures", you not only help us gauge the effectiveness of our efforts but also contribute to the collective knowledge and growth of our community of readers.

How You Can Help

We kindly invite you to take a moment to share your thoughts on "Mastering Business Structures", by leaving a review on your preferred platform, whether it be Amazon, Goodreads, or any other book review website. Your review can be a few sentences or a detailed analysis-every contribution is greatly appreciated.

What to Consider in Your Review

1. Did the book provide clear and actionable insights into different structures?
2. Were you able to make informed decisions regarding your business's legal framework and financial efficiency?
3. Did you find the strategies and recommendations for maximizing profits and securing growth practical and applicable to your business.
4. How did the book compare to other resources you've encountered on similar topics?

Thank You for Your Support

Your support means the world to us, and we genuinely appreciate your time and effort in sharing your feedback. Together, we can continue to empower entrepreneurs and business leaders worldwide to achieve their goals and unlock their full potential.

Scan the QR Code, if you would like leave a Review

Warm Regards,

Aaron & Darlene McCray

DA Affiliates 2

Chapter 5

Sole Proprietorship: The Seed of Business Success

In the tapestry of the entrepreneurial realm, the sole proprietorship stands not merely as a structure but as a testament to the raw spirit of individual ambition. This form, in its essence, captures the allure of business at its most fundamental — where a single soul takes the helm, navigating the tumultuous waters of the market with a blend of personal vision and relentless pursuit. Within this domain, stories of triumph and tribulation intertwine, offering a rich narrative of what it means to build, from the ground up, with one's own hands and heart.

5.1 Sole Proprietor Success Stories

Journey of Successful Sole Proprietors

The path to success for sole proprietors often mirrors the growth of a well-tended garden. Much like the gardener who selects the right seed, plants it in fertile soil, and nurtures it through seasons of both sunshine and storm, the sole proprietor begins with an idea — a seed. They plant this seed in the market, tending to it with dedication, strategy, and an unwavering resolve to see it flourish. This journey, fraught with challenges, requires not just hard work but a keen understanding of the landscape, a meticulous attention to the needs of one's burgeoning enterprise, and an adaptive strategy that ensures growth despite the odds.

Challenges Overcome

The road for sole proprietors is often paved with obstacles that test their resolve and ingenuity. A common hurdle is access to capital. Without the backing of partners or investors, sole proprietors must often rely on personal savings or loans, making the initial stages of business growth a tightrope walk of financial prudence. Additionally, the burden of wearing multiple hats — from product development to marketing, sales, and customer service — can stretch the capabilities and energies of any one person thin. Overcoming these challenges demands not just resilience but creativity in problem-solving, whether through leveraging digital tools to streamline operations or finding unique ways to engage and expand one's customer base.

Critical Success Factors

For sole proprietors, identifying and serving a niche market has proven time and again to be a cornerstone of success. This strategy, which allows for a focused approach to solving specific problems for a well-defined audience, enables sole proprietors to carve out a space for themselves even in crowded markets. Coupled with an unwavering commitment to customer service excellence, this focus ensures that sole proprietors can build a loyal customer base, turning first-time buyers into lifelong patrons. The personal touch, the ability to listen and adapt to customer needs swiftly, becomes the sole proprietor's strongest asset, distinguishing their offerings in a way that larger entities often struggle to replicate.

Transition to Other Structures

The evolution of a successful sole proprietorship

often reaches a juncture where growth necessitates a transformation. This transition, whether to an LLC, a partnership, or a corporation, marks a pivotal moment in the business's lifecycle, enabling it to scale operations, diversify its risk profile, and tap into new funding avenues. A prime example can be seen in small retail businesses that, after establishing a strong local presence and loyal customer base, opt to incorporate as a means to expand their footprint, both physically and online. This strategic shift, while significant, is a natural progression, enabling the business to harness new opportunities for growth while safeguarding the entrepreneurial spirit that fueled its initial success.

Interactive Element: Reflection on Growth and Structure

Reflection Exercise: **Are You Ready for a Transition?**

This exercise invites sole proprietors to reflect on their business's current stage and consider if a structural transition might be the next step in their growth journey.

1. **Assess Your Growth:** Reflect on your business's growth in the past year. Have you outgrown your current operational capacity?
2. **Consider Your Financial Health:** Analyze your financial standing. Is access to capital becoming a bottleneck for further expansion?
3. **Evaluate Your Market Position:** Look at your market position. Have you identified new opportunities that require a more robust operational or financial structure to capitalize on?

Review Your Risk Profile: Consider the risks you're

currently facing. Would a change in business structure provide better protection for your personal assets and offer more stability for the business? This reflection is not merely an exercise but a strategic pause, offering sole proprietors a moment to survey the terrain they've traversed and envision the path that lies ahead. With careful consideration, the decision to transition can mark the beginning of a new chapter, one where the foundations laid by the sole proprietor serve as a springboard for greater achievements and broader horizons.

5.2   LLCs in Action: Diverse Examples

The versatility of Limited Liability Companies (LLCs) is vividly illustrated through a mosaic of success stories spanning across industries, from tech startups to artisanal cafes. Each narrative not only serves as a testament to the structure's adaptability but also as a blueprint for navigating the intricate dance of entrepreneurship within this flexible framework.

In the realm of technology, a small app development firm initially operated with a lean team and modest resources. The choice of an LLC structure allowed for a streamlined approach to managing their operations while safeguarding personal assets. This protective shell was crucial as they ventured into the competitive app market, where legal challenges over intellectual property rights loom large. The operational agility of the LLC enabled the firm to pivot quickly in response to market feedback, iterating on their product in real-time without the encumbrance of cumbersome corporate formalities. This agility, coupled with the protection offered by the

LLC structure, provided a fertile ground for innovation and risk-taking, propelling the app from a niche offering to a staple on digital devices.

In contrast, the story of a boutique organic skincare line underscores the LLC's capacity to nurture ventures rooted in personal passion and commitment to sustainable practices. The founders, motivated by a vision to offer ethically sourced and produced products, found in the LLC structure the ideal framework for their operation. It allowed them to establish solid supplier partnerships and build a loyal customer base, anchored on the transparency and integrity of their business practices. The LLC facilitated these relationships, offering a structure that was flexible enough to accommodate their ethical sourcing requirements while providing the legal and financial scaffolding necessary to build a robust brand in the competitive beauty industry.

Navigating the complexities of growth and market expansion presents a universal challenge, yet for LLCs, these hurdles often become stages for demonstrating strategic acumen. A gourmet food truck, operating under the LLC umbrella, illustrates this adeptness. Initially catering to a local clientele, the business saw potential for expansion but faced the dual challenges of regulatory compliance and market penetration. The LLC structure facilitated a strategic expansion, allowing the owners to compartmentalize operations, manage risks effectively, and tap into new markets with agility. By creating separate LLCs for each truck, they minimized exposure and optimized operational efficiency, turning regulatory hurdles into stepping stones for growth.

The innovative use of the LLC structure to gain competitive advantages and achieve business goals is perhaps most strikingly displayed in the realm of renewable energy. A startup focusing on solar panel installations embraced the LLC model, not just for its liability protection and operational flexibility, but for the strategic partnerships it enabled. The structure allowed the company to forge alliances with manufacturers and finance institutions, crafting deals that would have been untenable under more rigid business forms. These partnerships were instrumental in developing unique financing options for clients, making solar installations accessible to a broader demographic and catapulting the startup to the forefront of the green energy movement.

Each of these tales, diverse in their settings and protagonists, converges on a common theme — the LLC as a dynamic vessel for entrepreneurial ambition. Whether navigating the treacherous waters of tech innovation, championing sustainability in the beauty industry, expanding the reach of culinary delights, or pioneering solutions in renewable energy, the LLC stands as a beacon of flexibility, protection, and growth potential. These narratives not only illuminate the path for future entrepreneurs but also underscore the transformative power of strategic structure selection in the journey to business success.

5.3 Innovative Partnerships Leading to Growth

In the realm where ambitions intertwine and collective endeavors shape the future, innovative partnerships stand as monuments to human ingenuity and collaborative spirit. These alliances, born out of strategic foresight and nurtured through shared visions, not only accelerate business growth but redefine the boundaries of what's achievable. Through a tapestry of narratives, we witness the transformative power of partnerships, where the amalgamation of diverse competencies and resources propels ventures into uncharted territories of success.

Strategic Partnership Success Stories

In the annals of business history, tales of strategic alliances that catalyzed exponential growth abound, serving as beacons for those seeking to tread the path of collaborative expansion.

Consider the fusion of a fledgling tech innovator with a seasoned manufacturing giant, a partnership that melded cutting-edge innovation with industrial prowess. This alliance, strategic in its core, leveraged the nimbleness and disruptive technology of the innovator against the manufacturing and distribution muscle of the giant. The result was a symbiotic growth that saw the innovator's solutions becoming integral to industries far beyond its initial scope, a testament to the foresight behind the partnership.

Collaborative Problem-Solving

The essence of partnerships often lies in their capacity to forge solutions to problems that seem insurmountable to individual entities. Through the lens of collaborative problem-solving, partnerships transcend mere alliances, becoming crucibles for innovation. A narrative that exemplifies this is the union of an environmental startup and a logistics firm, brought together by the shared goal of reducing carbon footprints in supply chains. By integrating the startup's green technologies with the logistics firm's network, they pioneered a model of sustainable logistics, addressing a critical industry challenge while setting new standards for environmental responsibility. This endeavor underscores how strategic partnerships can leverage collective intelligence to tackle complex issues, turning challenges into opportunities for growth and impact.

Partnership Agreements and Structures

The foundation of any successful partnership lies in its structure and the agreements that govern it, elements that ensure alignment and safeguard interests. Crafting these agreements demands a meticulous balance between vision and pragmatism, encapsulating the goals, roles, responsibilities, and benefits for each party. A noteworthy illustration of this balance can be found in the collaboration between a software company and a healthcare provider aiming to digitalize patient records. The partnership agreement delineated not just the developmental and operational roles but also the ownership of the resultant data and technologies, ensuring clarity and mutual benefit. Such agreements, when structured thoughtfully, serve as the backbone of partnerships, enabling seamless collaboration while protecting the interests of all involved.

Navigating Partnership Challenges

Despite the best-laid plans, partnerships may encounter turbulence, from divergent visions to operational discord. Navigating these challenges requires a blend of communication, flexibility, and a shared commitment to the partnership's core objectives. A case in point involves a partnership between a fashion brand and an e-commerce platform, aimed at expanding the brand's online presence. Initial disagreements on branding and customer engagement strategies threatened to derail the collaboration. However, through open communication and a willingness to adapt, both parties found common ground, aligning their strategies with the shared goal of maximizing online sales while maintaining brand integrity. This resolution highlights the critical role of effective communication and compromise in overcoming partnership challenges, ensuring that the alliance remains a conduit for growth and innovation.

In the panorama of innovative partnerships, these narratives not only illuminate the path to collaborative success but also emphasize the strategic, operational, and relational facets that underpin such alliances. From the strategic alignment that seeds growth to the collaborative problem-solving that fosters innovation, the structuring of agreements that ensure mutual benefit, and the adept navigation of challenges, partnerships emerge as powerful engines for business expansion and transformation. In this confluence of visions and competencies, partnerships not only lead to growth but redefine what businesses can achieve together, marking a new epoch in the saga of entrepreneurial endeavor.

5.4 Corporations: From Startup to Scaleup

In the landscape of business evolution, the transformative journey from a fledgling startup to a robust scaleup within the corporate structure unfolds with a narrative rich in strategic pivots, milestones, and an indomitable pursuit of growth. This passage, marked by the meticulous orchestration of resources, ingenuity in overcoming hurdles, and the strategic leverage of corporate advantages, presents a compelling blueprint for scaling success. Corporate Success Journeys

The inception of a corporation often starts with an idea potent enough to disrupt markets, yet it's the execution of this idea, through the scaffoldings of a corporate structure, that heralds true transformation. The initial phase sees founders laying the groundwork—meticulous market research, product development, and the establishment of key operational processes. Yet, it's the subsequent stages of growth that test the mettle and vision of these enterprises. The narrative of a technology firm that pivoted from a modest software solution provider to a global leader in cloud-based services encapsulates this evolution. Initial successes provided a solid base, but it was the strategic scaling—both in product offerings and geographic reach—that catapulted the corporation into new realms of success, utilizing the corporate structure to its full advantage by facilitating investments, attracting talent, and expanding operational capacity.

Strategic Decisions and Milestones

Navigating the growth trajectory of a corporation involves a series of calculated decisions and milestones that serve as stepping stones to scale. Significant among these is the pursuit of financing rounds, an endeavor that transforms the capital landscape of the corporation, infusing it with the resources needed for aggressive expansion. For many, the initial public offering (IPO) stands as a pivotal milestone, not just for the capital it brings but for the legitimacy and market presence it confers. A biotech firm's journey from a research-focused startup to a publicly traded entity underscores the strategic cadence of such financing milestones — seed funding to Series A through D, and finally, the IPO — each step meticulously planned to balance dilution with the necessity of growth capital.

Challenges and Solutions

The path of scaling is fraught with challenges that test the resilience and adaptability of corporations. Market penetration efforts often encounter stiff resistance from established players, necessitating innovative go-to-market strategies that leverage the corporation's structure for competitive advantage. Regulatory compliance emerges as another common hurdle, especially for corporations operating across multiple jurisdictions. The adept handling of these challenges involves a blend of strategic foresight and operational agility. A corporation specializing in renewable energy solutions navigated these waters by adopting a dual strategy of alliances with local partners for market entry and a proactive engagement with regulatory bodies, turning potential obstacles into opportunities for market leadership and advocacy for favorable regulatory frameworks.

Innovative solutions to operational scalability challenges also underscore the corporation's journey. The transition from a centralized to a decentralized operational model, facilitated by the corporate structure, enables effective management of expanded operations while preserving agility. The adoption of cutting-edge technologies for process automation and data analytics further empowers corporations to scale efficiently, managing complexities that accompany growth without succumbing to inefficiency. Lessons for Aspiring Entrepreneurs

For those at the helm of nascent enterprises, the corporate success stories offer not just inspiration but tangible lessons in leveraging structure for growth. The importance of strategic planning cannot be overstated, with a clear vision for the company's growth trajectory serving as a compass for decision-making. Ensuring that the corporate structure is optimized for flexibility and scalability from the outset allows for smoother transitions through growth phases, adapting to challenges and seizing opportunities with agility.

The strategic approach to financing, balancing the infusion of capital with the preservation of control and vision, emerges as a critical lesson. Entrepreneurs learn the art of negotiation, understanding that each round of financing is not just a transaction but a partnership that shapes the future of the enterprise. Furthermore, the significance of building a robust corporate culture — one that fosters innovation, agility, and a collective pursuit of goals — becomes a cornerstone for sustainable growth. This culture acts as the glue that binds the enterprise together, ensuring that as the corporation scales, it retains the core values and mission that propelled its initial success.

Lastly, the journey teaches the value of resilience and adaptability, qualities embodied in the corporate structure itself. Entrepreneurs come to understand that challenges and obstacles are not just barriers but opportunities for refinement, strategic pivots, and, ultimately, growth. The corporate journey from startup to scaleup, rich in its complexity and marked by strategic ingenuity, stands as a testament to the potential that lies in leveraging the corporate structure for building enduring, scalable enterprises.

5.5   S-Corp Case Studies: Maximizing Tax Benefits

In the nuanced world of business structures, the S-Corporation stands out for its unique blend of corporate identity with pass-through taxation advantages. This hybrid nature has attracted a diverse array of businesses, each leveraging the S-Corp status to align closely with their strategic fiscal objectives while navigating the intricate landscape of operational adjustments and regulatory compliance. Through the lens of case studies, we uncover the motivations behind the selection of S-Corp status, the tax planning strategies that have yielded substantial savings, and the operational maneuvers that underpin the successful leveraging of this distinctive structure.

Businesses venturing into the S-Corp domain often do so driven by a clear vision to capitalize on the tax benefits while maintaining the operational flexibility akin to a partnership. A bakery, transformed from a local favorite into a wholesale supplier, illustrates this transition, propelled by the desire to mitigate the tax burden while preparing for an exponential growth trajectory. The election to S-Corp status was not merely a fiscal decision but a strategic move to position the bakery favorably in a competitive market, enabling it to reinvest savings into expanding its production capacity and distribution network. This strategic pivot underscored the bakery's commitment to growth, facilitated by the tax efficiency intrinsic to the S-Corp structure. The tax planning landscape for S-Corporations is rich with strategies designed to optimize fiscal outcomes. One such approach involves the meticulous structuring of salary and dividend distributions to shareholders, a balance that seeks to minimize self-employment taxes while ensuring compliance with IRS guidelines on reasonable compensation. A tech consultancy firm stands as a paragon in this realm, its meticulous planning resulting in significant tax savings that bolstered its bottom line. Through a calculated allocation between salaries and dividends, the firm not only complied with tax regulations but also maximized the income passed through to shareholders, showcasing the potent synergy between strategic tax planning and the operational dynamics of an S-Corp.

Operational adjustments are paramount for businesses seeking to fully harness the benefits of S-Corp status. These adjustments often entail a recalibration of internal processes and financial management practices to align with the requirements and advantages of the S-Corp framework. A notable instance is a manufacturing enterprise that restructured its operational model to facilitate more efficient asset management and cost allocation, directly impacting its fiscal health. The shift to an S-Corp necessitated a reevaluation of inventory practices, leading to a leaner, more cost-effective operation that capitalized on the tax advantages of the structure while enhancing operational efficiency.

Navigating the challenges inherent to the S-Corp status requires a blend of foresight, adaptability, and meticulous compliance with regulatory stipulations. The constraints on shareholder numbers and eligibility criteria pose a particular challenge, especially for businesses on a rapid growth trajectory or those with diverse investor bases. A digital marketing agency confronted this challenge head-on, deploying a strategy that involved selective investor engagement and a clear communication plan to manage shareholder expectations. This proactive approach ensured the agency remained within the bounds of S-Corp eligibility, preserving its tax advantages while continuing to attract the investment necessary for growth.

The journey through the S-Corp landscape, as illuminated by these case studies, reveals a structure that offers substantial benefits for businesses adept at navigating its complexities. From strategic tax planning that enhances fiscal health to operational adjustments that bolster efficiency, the S-Corp status presents a compelling option for businesses poised for growth. Yet, the pathway to leveraging this structure successfully is punctuated with challenges, from shareholder restrictions to compliance demands, each requiring a strategic response.

In reflecting on the narratives of businesses that have thrived under the S-Corp structure, a broader theme emerges — one that underscores the critical interplay between strategic planning, fiscal management, and regulatory compliance in the pursuit of business success.

These stories not only illuminate the potential advantages of the S-Corp status but also highlight the operational and strategic acumen necessary to navigate its complexities effectively. As we transition from these explorations, the insights gleaned here serve as a foundation for understanding the broader implications of business structure choices, paving the way for a deeper dive into the dynamics of financial management and growth strategies in the chapters to follow.

Chapter 6

Demystifying Legal Speak: A Guide for Entrepreneurs

In a landscape where every word can weigh as much as gold, the complex dialect of legal jargon often becomes the quicksand that entraps the unwary entrepreneur. This chapter aims to cut through the thicket, transforming the arcane into the accessible. Here, the focus is not just on unearthing the essence of commonly encountered legal terms but on embedding this newfound understanding into the practical soil of business operations.

6.1　Simplifying Complex Legal Jargon

Glossary of Common Legal Terms

At the heart of every informed decision lies understanding. For an entrepreneur, grappling with terms like "limited liability," "indemnification," or "proprietary information" without a solid grasp of their meanings is akin to navigating a dense fog. A glossary becomes an indispensable tool, a beacon through the mist. Consider "limited liability" — a term that underpins the very decision of choosing an LLC. It signifies protection; personal assets are shielded from business debts and lawsuits. This glossary, therefore, is more than a list; it's a bridge to making informed decisions.

Real-World Examples and Case Studies

Imagine a small café wrestling with the decision of

whether to structure as a sole proprietorship or an LLC. The café's owner, faced with the prospect of a lawsuit stemming from a slip-and-fall incident, discovers the protective embrace of "limited liability" under an LLC. This scenario, detailed in a case study, not only brings the term to life but also illustrates the tangible implications of legal structures on everyday business operations.

Visual Aids for Complex Concepts

Visual aids act as clarifiers in the murky waters of legal terminology. Charts comparing the tax implications of different business structures, or infographics outlining the steps to trademark a brand, translate abstract concepts into concrete visuals. These aids serve not just to inform but to empower, enabling entrepreneurs to visualize the pathways and implications of their decisions.

Interactive Tools for Applying Legal Terms

Interactive tools bring the practical application of legal terms into the hands of the entrepreneur. Imagine an online simulator that allows a business owner to input their specific parameters—number of owners, expected revenue, risk factors—and receive a recommendation for the most suitable legal structure. This tool not only demystifies the term "business structure" but also provides a personalized insight into its implications, making the abstract personal. In this chapter, the dense thicket of legal jargon is not merely cut away but transformed into a landscaped garden, where entrepreneurs can walk freely, empowered by understanding and equipped with the tools to apply this knowledge to their ventures. Through glossaries, real-world scenarios, visual aids, and interactive tools, the language of law becomes not an obstacle but an ally in the journey of business.

6.2   Strategies to Avoid Overwhelm in Structure Selection

In the labyrinth of legal structures available to the modern entrepreneur, the sheer breadth of choice can often paralyze rather than empower. The key to navigating this complex terrain lies not in the brute force of decision-making but in the elegance of a methodical approach, a measured step-by-step journey through the intricacies of legal frameworks designed to suit the unique fabric of each business. This pathway, delineated through a series of strategic interventions, promises not just clarity but confidence in the selection of a business structure that resonates with the core objectives and operational ethos of the enterprise.

Dissecting the Decision Process into Manageable Steps

The initiation of this journey requires a dissection of the decision-making process into its constituent steps, a methodical deconstruction that transforms an overwhelming choice into a series of manageable considerations. The first step anchors in self-reflection, a deep dive into the entrepreneur's values, ambitions, and the vision for the business. This introspection sets the stage for the subsequent analysis of business needs—financial, operational, and growth-oriented—layering a nuanced understanding of the venture's requirements over the foundational values established.

Following this introspection, the path leads to market analysis, an evaluation of the competitive landscape and regulatory environment that the business will navigate. This step not only informs the entrepreneur of the external factors influencing their venture but also aligns the business's operational needs with the realities of the market. The culmination of this process lies in a strategic alignment, a point where the entrepreneur's vision, the business's needs, and the market's demands converge, guiding the selection of a legal structure that supports robust growth, operational efficiency, and legal compliance.

Crafting a Questionnaire to Illuminate Core Business Needs

To illuminate the core needs of the business, a finely crafted questionnaire emerges as a tool of unparalleled utility. This instrument probes not just the surface-level desires of the entrepreneur but delves into the operational, financial, and strategic depths of the venture. Questions might span the spectrum from the expected trajectory of growth and the nature of customer interactions to the appetite for risk and the priorities in profit distribution. Each response adds a stroke to the portrait of the business, gradually revealing a picture that transcends the generic, highlighting the unique attributes and needs that will dictate the ideal legal structure.

Utilizing Comparative Tables to Elucidate Structural Distinctions In the quest for clarity, comparative tables stand as pillars of insight, transforming abstract distinctions between legal structures into tangible comparisons. These tables juxtapose critical attributes of each structure—liability protection, tax implications, operational flexibility, and scalability—against the backdrop of the business's identified needs. Through this comparative lens, the entrepreneur gains not just an understanding of the legal frameworks but a visual map of how each structure aligns with or diverges from their specific business requirements. This clarity, born from direct comparison, simplifies the complex, guiding the entrepreneur toward a structure that harmonizes with their operational ethos and strategic ambitions.

Seeking External Advice for Informed Direction

The journey towards selecting a business structure, while deeply personal, benefits immensely from the external perspectives of legal and financial advisors. These professionals, armed with years of experience and a nuanced understanding of both the legal landscape and market dynamics, offer insights that transcend the generic, providing tailored advice that resonates with the specific contours of the business. Consulting with these advisors becomes a crucial step in the decision-making process, a dialog that not only illuminates potential pitfalls and opportunities but also refines the entrepreneur's understanding of how each legal structure might shape the future of their venture.

In engaging with legal advisors, the entrepreneur taps into a wellspring of knowledge on compliance, liability, and the subtleties of legal protection, while financial advisors shed light on the fiscal implications of each structure, from tax obligations to fundraising capabilities. This collaborative exploration, enriched by external expertise, ensures that the decision is not just informed by personal vision and operational needs but is vetted through the lens of legal and financial viability.

In traversing the path to selecting a business structure, the entrepreneur embarks on a journey that is as much about self-discovery as it is about legal compliance and operational strategy.

Through a methodical approach that dissects the decision-making process, illuminates the core needs of the business, employs comparative analysis for clarity, and incorporates external expertise for depth, the choice of legal structure transforms from an overwhelming challenge into a strategic decision. This decision, grounded in a comprehensive understanding of both the business and the broader legal and financial landscape, sets the foundation for a venture that is not only legally sound and operationally efficient but poised for sustained growth and success.

6.3 Mitigating the Fear of Irreversible Mistakes

In the vast expanse of entrepreneurial decision-making, the specter of irreversible mistakes often looms large, casting long shadows over the pathways of growth and adaptation. This pervasive fear, while understandable, need not be a paralyzing force. At its core, the journey through business structuring and re-structuring is replete with opportunities for recalibration and renewal. The narrative that decisions, once made, are cast in stone is a myth that warrants dispelling. Instead, a dynamic perspective that views business structures as fluid, evolving entities offers a liberating vision, one where change is not just possible but often beneficial. The annals of business history are adorned with tales of ventures that, upon encountering crossroads, chose to reimagine their structural foundations, thereby unlocking new realms of potential. Consider, for instance, a tech startup initially registered as a partnership due to its founders' shared vision. As the startup expanded, the limitations of this structure in accommodating outside investments and facilitating scalable growth became apparent. The decision to transition to a corporate entity, fraught with apprehensions of complexity and loss of control, ultimately proved to be a catalyst for unprecedented growth, attracting venture capital and enabling global market penetration. This transformation underscores the principle that business structures, far from being static, are adaptable frameworks designed to support the venture's evolving landscape.

Central to navigating this terrain with confidence is the dual beacon of education and preparation. The quest for knowledge, an expedition into the intricacies of legal and financial implications of various business structures, equips the entrepreneur with the foresight to anticipate challenges and opportunities. This enlightenment is further enriched through consultations with experts, whose insights provide clarity and direction, illuminating the path through the fog of uncertainty. Engaging with legal advisors and financial consultants, entrepreneurs glean nuanced understandings of the implications of structural decisions, from tax ramifications to liability considerations, crafting a fortified foundation upon which to base informed choices.

In parallel, the cultivation of robust risk management strategies acts as a bulwark against potential missteps. The deployment of risk assessment tools, ranging from financial audits to operational reviews, enables businesses to identify vulnerabilities and preemptively address them. Insurance, in its myriad forms, from general liability to professional indemnity, offers a shield against unforeseen adversities, safeguarding the venture's financial health and operational continuity. This proactive stance towards risk management transforms potential liabilities into managed variables, instilling a sense of security and resilience within the entrepreneurial psyche.

Yet, perhaps the most potent antidote to the fear of irreversible mistakes is a lucid understanding of the process and implications of changing business structures. The legal landscape, with its statutes and regulations, provides mechanisms for transformation, from the reclassification of a sole proprietorship to an LLC to the evolution of an LLC into a corporation. Each step in this process, governed by legal protocols and procedural requirements, is a testament to the flexibility that underpins the business legal framework. By demystifying the steps involved, from filing the necessary documentation with state and federal agencies to addressing tax consequences and stakeholder communications, the path to structural change is clarified. Entrepreneurs discover that the journey through restructuring is not a treacherous traverse but a strategic maneuver, one that aligns the business more closely with its aspirational trajectory.

This recalibrated perspective, viewing decisions not as final edicts but as iterative steps in the venture's progression, imbues entrepreneurs with the courage to embrace change. The realization that structures can evolve in tandem with the business's growth trajectory dissolves the paralysis induced by fear, replacing it with a proactive stance towards adaptation and growth. In this light, the decision-making process transcends the avoidance of mistakes, embracing instead the pursuit of alignment, efficiency, and scalability.

The essence of mitigating the fear of irreversible mistakes lies not in the illusion of perfection but in the embrace of adaptability and informed decision-making. Through the tapestry of stories that celebrate successful transformations, the beacon of education and preparation, the shield of risk management strategies, and the clarity of understanding the legalities of change, entrepreneurs are equipped to navigate the complexities of business structuring with confidence. This paradigm, where change is not only possible but often a harbinger of growth, offers a liberating vision for the entrepreneurial journey, one where the fear of missteps is replaced with the anticipation of possibilities, and the narrative of irreversibility is reimagined as a story of evolution and renewal.

6.4   Staying Informed: Legal and Regulatory Updates

In the evolving tapestry of the entrepreneurial landscape, the constant shifts in legal and regulatory frameworks pose a formidable challenge, requiring businesses to remain ever-vigilant and adaptable. This dynamic environment, where legal amendments and regulatory adjustments are par for the course, underscores the necessity for entrepreneurs to cultivate a proactive stance towards compliance. Navigating this terrain with acuity hinges on the entrepreneur's ability to tap into a reservoir of up-to-date information, leveraging a blend of resources, technology, professional networks, and internal audits to maintain a pulse on the legal heartbeat that underscores business operations.

At the forefront of this informational arsenal stand newsletters, websites, and agencies dedicated to disseminating current legal information, serving as sentinels on the lookout for regulatory shifts. These platforms range from government websites offering bulletins on statutory changes to industry-specific newsletters that curate legal updates with a sectoral lens. For instance, an entrepreneur in the fintech space might subscribe to newsletters from regulatory bodies like the Financial Conduct Authority, alongside frequent visits to technology law forums, ensuring a panoramic view of the legal landscape. This curated approach to information gathering allows for a targeted consumption of relevant updates, minimizing noise while maximizing relevance and applicability.

Parallel to these traditional conduits of information flow, technology emerges as a potent ally in the quest to stay informed. A plethora of apps and software solutions have burgeoned, designed with the express purpose of alerting businesses to legal changes that hold implications for their operations. These digital tools, equipped with algorithms capable of sifting through the morass of legal documents, provide tailored alerts based on the business's specific parameters — be it industry, size, or geographic location. By integrating such technology into the operational workflow, entrepreneurs can ensure a continuous stream of pertinent legal updates, delivered with precision and timeliness, thereby streamlining the process of staying abreast of changes that necessitate adjustments in compliance strategies. In tandem with these digital and informational resources, the value of professional networking in keeping informed cannot be overstated. Industry associations and professional conferences serve as vibrant ecosystems for the exchange of knowledge, insights, and experiences, often illuminating the practical implications of legal changes in a manner that documents and bulletins cannot capture. By embedding themselves within these networks, entrepreneurs gain access to a collective wisdom, forged through the diverse experiences of peers who navigate the same regulatory landscapes. This communal pool of knowledge acts as a compass, guiding businesses through the intricacies of compliance with a nuanced understanding of not just what the legal changes entail, but how they manifest in day-to-day operations.

Beyond external sources of information and networking lies the cornerstone of compliance — internal audits. Regular audits, conducted with a lens towards identifying potential regulatory oversights, serve as a critical self-check mechanism, ensuring that the business's operational practices remain in lockstep with legal requirements. These audits, whether performed by internal teams or through the engagement of external consultants, delve into every facet of the business, from financial transactions and employment practices to data management and consumer protection. By instituting a regimen of periodic audits, businesses can preemptively address compliance issues, rectifying potential infractions before they escalate into legal challenges. This proactive approach to compliance not only safeguards the business against regulatory pitfalls but also instills a culture of accountability and diligence within the organization.

In this vigilant pursuit of compliance, where the landscape is perpetually in flux, the entrepreneur's toolkit expands to encompass a diverse array of resources. From the curated insights of newsletters and the tailored alerts of technological tools to the collective wisdom of professional networks and the introspective lens of internal audits, this arsenal equips businesses to navigate the legal complexities with informed confidence. Through this multifaceted strategy, maintaining compliance transcends the reactive, evolving into a dynamic process of continuous adaptation and proactive engagement with the legal frameworks that shape the entrepreneurial world. In the intricate dance of business operations, where each step is guided by the unseen hand of regulatory mandates, staying informed emerges not just as a strategy, but as a fundamental ethos, embedding within the business a resilience that fortifies its journey through the ever-changing terrain of legal and regulatory landscapes.

6.5   Translating Theory into Actionable Steps

The chasm between theoretical knowledge and its practical application in the realm of business structure can seem vast and daunting. Yet, it is in the bridging of this gap where the true essence of entrepreneurial acumen comes to light. The journey from conceptual understanding to tangible action necessitates a scaffold of resources designed to distill complex theories into digestible, implementable strategies.

Providing Templates and Checklists Templates and checklists serve as the architect's tools in the construction of a business's legal framework. Their utility lies not merely in their ability to organize thoughts but in their power to transform abstract concepts into clear, actionable tasks. A template for evaluating the suitability of various business structures, for instance, guides the entrepreneur through a series of criteria—risk tolerance, tax preferences, growth ambitions—culminating in a recommendation tailored to the specific contours of their venture. Similarly, a checklist for the steps required to form an LLC acts as a roadmap, ensuring no critical component is overlooked in the transition from theory to practice.

Incorporating Case Studies with Actionable Insights

The potency of a case study lies in its ability to weave theory into the narrative fabric of real-world scenarios, offering a dual lens of hindsight and foresight. An exploration into a startup's evolution from a sole proprietorship to a multinational corporation, for instance, sheds light on the strategic considerations, challenges, and pivots that marked its journey. These narratives are more than stories; they are repositories of wisdom, offering actionable insights on navigating regulatory hurdles, leveraging tax advantages, and scaling operations. Each case study serves as a beacon, guiding entrepreneurs through the murky waters of decision-making, illuminated by the successes and stumbles of those who have navigated similar paths.

Offering Access to Online Simulations

In the dynamic arena of business, where variables shift with the market winds, the ability to anticipate and adapt is invaluable. Online simulations, mirroring the complexities of business structuring decisions under varying scenarios, provide a virtual sandbox for experimentation. Entrepreneurs can explore the ramifications of choosing an S-corporation over an LLC, for instance, under different tax regimes, growth rates, and funding landscapes. These simulations, grounded in the principles of game theory and economic modeling, enable a hands-on approach to strategic planning, allowing for the exploration of outcomes without the real-world risks.

Encouraging Feedback Loops for Refinement

The pursuit of perfection in business structuring is a mirage; the goal, instead, is continuous improvement. Feedback loops, established through mentorship and peer review systems, act as the crucible for this refinement. By inviting critique and guidance from seasoned entrepreneurs and advisors, business owners can gain insights into the nuances of their chosen structures, identifying areas for optimization. This cyclical process of implementation, review, and adjustment ensures that the business structure remains not only compliant with current regulations but also aligned with the venture's evolving strategy and market position.

In this landscape where theory and action converge, the entrepreneur is equipped not merely with knowledge but with the instruments of implementation. Templates and checklists translate abstract concepts into concrete plans, case studies offer the wisdom of experience, simulations provide a risk-free environment for strategic exploration, and feedback loops ensure continuous alignment with both regulatory mandates and business ambitions. Through these mechanisms, the leap from theoretical understanding to practical application is not a leap at all but a series of measured steps, each grounded in the reality of business operations and aimed at fostering growth, innovation, and resilience.

As we draw this exploration to its close, the journey from the realms of theory to the tangible landscapes of business structuring reveals itself to be less about the distance traveled and more about the depth of understanding gained. The transformation of complex legal theories into actionable steps for entrepreneurs represents not just a bridging of knowledge but a fusion, where strategic insight meets practical application. This synthesis, enriched by the tools of templates, case studies, simulations, and feedback, equips business owners with the clarity and confidence to navigate the intricacies of legal structures, ensuring that their ventures are not only compliant and efficient but poised for growth and adaptation in the ever-evolving market landscape.

As we turn our gaze forward, the path ahead beckons with the promise of further exploration into the strategies that underpin successful business operations, ensuring that the foundation laid here serves as a springboard for the continued evolution and success of entrepreneurial endeavors.

Chapter 7

Navigating the Crossroads: LLC vs. Sole Proprietorship

In the tapestry of business structure choices, two threads often pull with equal tension: the LLC and the Sole Proprietorship. Each holds its allure, woven from the fibers of liability, taxation, ambition, and regulation. The decision between the two is not a mere flip of a coin but a careful consideration of how each aligns with the entrepreneur's current standing and future aspirations. This chapter delves into this critical decision, shedding light on key areas where these structures diverge and guiding you through the intricate considerations necessary to make an informed choice.

7.1 LLC or Sole Proprietorship: Making the Choice

Liability and Taxation: A Balancing Act

The distinction between an LLC and a Sole Proprietorship becomes stark when viewed through the lens of liability and taxation. For the Sole Proprietor, the business and the individual are legally inseparable, a simple arrangement that allows for direct control but places personal assets at risk. The LLC, in contrast, erects a wall between business debts and personal property, a safeguard that comes with the complexity of adherence to more structured operating procedures.

Visual Element: Chart Comparing Liability and Taxation

An infographic clearly delineates how liability and taxation differ between an LLC and a Sole Proprietorship, using icons and arrows to demonstrate the flow of financial responsibility and the separation (or lack thereof) between personal and business assets.

Growth Ambitions and Professional Perception

Ambitions for growth often tip the scales in favor of forming an LLC. This structure not only fosters a perception of professionalism and commitment but also opens doors to funding opportunities otherwise barred to Sole Proprietorships. Investors and banks, wary of the blurred lines between personal and business finances in Sole Proprietorships, are more inclined to engage with the distinct legal entity of an LLC. This distinction becomes crucial in industries where the scale of operations and the need for investment capital are pivotal to advancement.

The Role of State Regulations

State-specific laws further complicate this decision, with some states offering incentives for LLCs through reduced fees or simplified filing processes. Conversely, other states may impose hefty annual taxes on LLCs, diminishing the appeal of the liability protection they offer. This geographical variation demands that entrepreneurs not only consult local regulations but also consider how interstate expansion might be affected by these legal landscapes.

Interactive Element: State Regulation Checklist

A comprehensive checklist that prompts the

entrepreneur to research and note down state-specific regulations affecting LLCs and Sole Proprietorships. This tool guides the user through key legal considerations, ensuring no critical regulatory factor is overlooked in making their decision.

Operational Complexity and Paperwork

The day-to-day operation of a business under these structures can differ as markedly as night and day. The Sole Proprietorship offers simplicity, with minimal paperwork and the freedom to make unilateral decisions. This ease of operation, however, comes at the cost of less structural support for scaling operations. LLCs, while necessitating a more complex setup and ongoing compliance with formalities like annual reports and organizational meetings, provide a framework that supports growth through clear operational roles and responsibilities.

Textual Element: Real-Life Scenario: Cafe Expansion

A scenario unfolds detailing the owner of a successful local café contemplating expansion. Initially operating as a Sole Proprietorship, the owner faces the decision of transitioning to an LLC to better accommodate the complexities of managing multiple locations, hiring additional staff, and attracting investors. This real-life example highlights not just the operational considerations but also the emotional and strategic deliberations that accompany such a pivotal business decision.

In navigating the crossroads between an LLC and a Sole Proprietorship, the entrepreneur must weigh these considerations with both the mind of a strategist and the heart of a visionary. The choice embodies not just a legal formality but a declaration of the business's identity and the path it seeks to tread. As this chapter unfolds, it aims to serve not as a prescriptive directive but as a compass, empowering you with the knowledge to choose the structure that aligns with your present realities and future aspirations, ensuring that the foundation upon which you build is not only solid but capable of supporting the weight of your dreams.

7.2   Decoding Pass-through Taxation

In the labyrinth of fiscal responsibilities that entwine the essence of business operations, pass-through taxation emerges as an oasis for certain entities, imbuing them with a fiscal advantage that is as alluring as it is complex. This taxation paradigm, in its essence, enables profits and losses to permeate directly to the personal tax returns of the business owners, bypassing the entity itself and thus, eschewing the specter of double taxation that haunts corporations. The simplicity of this concept belies the intricate dance of numbers and legal stipulations that govern its application, mandating a meticulous examination of its facets.

The beacon that guides small business owners towards pass-through taxation is the allure of streamlined tax processes. By allowing profits and losses to flow directly to their personal tax returns, entrepreneurs find solace in a simplified tax preparation process, unburdened by the complexities that corporate tax filings entail. This direct reporting mechanism not only eases the administrative load but also aligns the business's fiscal outcomes with the personal financial landscape of the owner, creating a seamless financial narrative that encompasses both personal and business realms.

Yet, the embrace of pass-through taxation is not universal across all business structures. The legal entities that bask in its benefits are delineated by specific criteria, with sole proprietorships, partnerships, and S-corporations standing as the privileged recipients. Each of these structures, by virtue of their legal design, qualifies for pass-through treatment, yet they are bound by a tapestry of conditions that dictate the extent and manner of its application. The sole proprietorship, in its solitary endeavor, naturally aligns with the principles of pass-through taxation, as does the partnership with its collective ownership. The S-corporation, however, walks a fine line, maintaining its corporate identity while adhering to stringent eligibility criteria that allow it to partake in the pass-through advantage.

This fiscal mechanism, while a boon, casts a shadow on personal tax rates and liabilities, introducing a complexity that demands strategic navigation. The confluence of business profits with personal income has the potential to elevate the owner's tax bracket, subjecting them to a higher tax rate that could erode the financial benefits of pass-through taxation. This potential escalation in tax obligations underscores the need for a nuanced understanding of how business operations impact personal finances, emphasizing the importance of strategic financial planning to mitigate adverse tax consequences.

In the realm of pass-through entities, the crucible of success lies in adept financial management and tax planning. Entrepreneurs are tasked with crafting a fiscal strategy that not only capitalizes on the benefits of pass-through taxation but also safeguards against its pitfalls. This strategy encompasses a broad spectrum of considerations, from the meticulous allocation of profits and losses to the judicious management of deductible expenses and investment decisions. The goal is to achieve a harmonious balance that leverages the tax advantages of pass-through taxation while minimizing its impact on personal tax liabilities.

One of the strategic maneuvers in this fiscal ballet involves the discerning use of deductions and credits, carefully selected to offset taxable income and thus, mitigate the tax burden. This approach requires a deep dive into the tax code, identifying opportunities for deductions that align with the business's operations and growth initiatives. Similarly, the strategic timing of income and expenses, adjusting the recognition of revenue and the undertaking of significant expenditures, becomes a pivotal tool in managing tax obligations. This temporal adjustment allows business owners to exert influence over their taxable income, strategically deferring or accelerating income and expenses to optimize their tax position.

Another facet of strategic financial management in pass-through entities is the proactive planning for capital investments and business expansion. The decisions surrounding these pivotal moments are imbued with tax implications, demanding a comprehensive analysis that considers both immediate fiscal impacts and long-term tax strategies. Entrepreneurs must weigh the benefits of reinvesting profits back into the business against the potential tax savings of distributing those profits directly. This deliberation extends to the realm of retirement planning, where contributions to qualified plans offer both a mechanism for future financial security and a tool for tax mitigation.

The landscape of pass-through taxation, with its intricate interplay of benefits and considerations, beckons small business owners to embark on a journey of strategic financial planning. This journey, marked by the meticulous management of finances and taxes, demands not only a grasp of the legal intricacies that define pass-through entities but also an acute awareness of the broader fiscal implications. Through this lens, the decision to embrace a pass-through entity transcends mere tax considerations, evolving into a strategic choice that shapes the financial trajectory of the business and its owner. In this realm, where personal and business finances converge under the auspices of pass-through taxation, the art of strategic financial management emerges as the linchpin of fiscal success, guiding entrepreneurs through the complexities of taxation towards the realization of their business aspirations.

7.3 The Process of Changing Business Structures

In the dynamic arena of business, evolution is not just a choice but a necessity. The decision to alter the foundational structure of a company often marks a pivotal point in its lifecycle, reflecting not merely a shift in legal designation but a deeper realignment with its growth trajectory and strategic objectives. This metamorphosis, while imbued with the promise of new opportunities, is navigated through a terrain rife with legal intricacies, financial recalibrations, and operational reconfigurations. The initiation of this transformation is typically spurred by a confluence of factors, ranging from the quest for enhanced scalability to the imperative for more robust liability protection. The catalysts for structural change are as varied as the businesses themselves. For some, the impetus is the expansion beyond the limitations of a sole proprietorship, seeking the financial allure and professional veneer of a corporation or LLC. For others, the drive towards change is rooted in the need for a more favorable tax regime or the desire to insulate personal assets from business liabilities. This decision, however, is not made in isolation but is the culmination of a nuanced assessment of how each structure aligns with the company's operational ethos and future aspirations.

Embarking on this journey requires meticulous planning and a keen awareness of the legal, financial, and operational ramifications. The initial step in this process is often the most daunting—the legal transition. This phase demands a thorough audit of existing agreements, contracts, and obligations to ensure they are in consonance with the new structure. The legal paperwork, a labyrinth of forms and filings, varies significantly from one jurisdiction to another, mandating a careful review of state-specific requirements. This legal odyssey extends beyond mere paperwork, encompassing a reevaluation of the company's tax status, a reassessment of its compliance with industry regulations, and a reconfiguration of its ownership and governance structures.

Simultaneously, the financial landscape of the company undergoes a profound transformation. This metamorphosis entails not just a reassessment of tax obligations under the new structure but also a recalibration of financial systems and processes. The implications for cash flow management, capital allocation, and fundraising strategies are profound, requiring a strategic approach to navigate the fiscal complexities of the transition. This financial shift is accompanied by an operational upheaval, as the company adjusts its internal workflows, reporting lines, and management practices to align with the demands of the new structure.

The timing of this transition is a critical consideration, one that demands a strategic calculus that balances the urgency of change with the readiness of the organization to embrace it. Optimal timing often coincides with natural points of business renewal — perhaps the close of a fiscal year or the culmination of a major project — moments that lend themselves to reflection and recalibration. Planning for this transition involves not just the logistical coordination of legal filings and operational adjustments but also the careful management of stakeholder expectations, ensuring a seamless shift in the company's public persona and internal dynamics.

Guidance from seasoned professionals becomes indispensable in this complex process. Legal advisors, with their deep understanding of corporate law, offer invaluable insights into the nuances of the transition, ensuring compliance with legal statutes and minimizing exposure to liability. Financial consultants, versed in the art of fiscal management, provide strategic counsel on navigating the tax implications of the new structure, optimizing financial performance through the turbulence of change. This professional support extends beyond mere advisory services, offering a strategic partnership that guides the company through the intricacies of the transition, ensuring that each step is taken with a clear understanding of its implications.

This process of changing business structures, then, is not a mere administrative task but a strategic endeavor that touches every facet of the company's operations. It demands a holistic approach that encompasses legal compliance, financial optimization, and operational agility, guided by professional expertise and strategic foresight. The journey through this transformation, while complex, offers the promise of aligning the company more closely with its strategic objectives, unlocking new avenues for growth, and fortifying its foundations for the challenges and opportunities that lie ahead.

7.4 Keeping Up with Business Regulation Changes

The fluidity of the regulatory environment encapsulates a relentless force, molding the operational landscapes within which businesses must navigate. This dynamism, characterized by frequent adjustments at federal, state, and local levels, demands a vigilant posture from entrepreneurs. Proactive engagement with these fluctuations is not merely advisable but imperative for maintaining the legal and operational integrity of a business. The essence of this vigilance lies in the meticulous monitoring of legal changes, a practice that ensures enterprises remain aligned with the latest regulatory requirements, thus safeguarding against the pitfalls of non-compliance.

Proactive Monitoring of Legal Changes Across Jurisdictions

The task of staying abreast of regulatory shifts necessitates a multi-faceted approach, one that spans the spectrum of governmental tiers. In this endeavor, the entrepreneur assumes the role of a vigilant sentinel, attuned to the nuances of legal changes that emerge from the labyrinth of legislative halls. This attentiveness to the shifting sands of regulation forms the bedrock upon which businesses can construct strategies that are not only compliant but resilient. The implications of these regulatory dynamics extend far beyond the mere adherence to statutes; they influence strategic decisions, operational methodologies, and market engagements, rendering the monitoring of legal changes a cornerstone of strategic business management.

Leveraging Technology and Automation for Efficient Regulatory Tracking

In the arsenal available to entrepreneurs for this task, technology and automation emerge as potent allies. The advent of software solutions and online services, engineered to track and report on legal developments, represents a paradigm shift in how businesses engage with the regulatory environment. These digital tools, with their capacity to filter and funnel relevant information based on customized parameters, offer a streamlined avenue for regulatory monitoring. This technological embrace not only alleviates the burden of manual tracking but also injects a level of precision and timeliness into the process, enabling businesses to respond with agility to regulatory changes. The deployment of these solutions, therefore, transcends mere convenience, positioning technology as a pivotal element in the strategic toolkit of the modern entrepreneur.

Fostering Collaboration and Information Sharing Within Professional Networks

Parallel to the technological approach stands the human dimension of regulatory engagement, embodied in the collaborative spaces of business networks and forums. These congregations of entrepreneurial minds offer a rich tapestry of experiences and insights, serving as a collective repository of knowledge on navigating the regulatory landscapes. Within these forums, the sharing of updates, strategies, and compliance tips transforms into a communal endeavor, enriching the individual entrepreneur's understanding with the breadth of collective experience. This collaborative ethos not only amplifies the reach of regulatory intelligence but also cultivates a culture of shared vigilance, where the burden of staying informed is distributed across the network, enhancing the overall resilience of the entrepreneurial community.

Institutionalizing Regular Legal Consultations to Preempt Compliance Issues

Anchoring these strategies in a framework of professional oversight, regular consultations with legal advisors stand as a critical practice. These engagements, characterized by a deep dive into the legal intricacies of the business's operations, provide a dual benefit. On one hand, they offer a mechanism for preemptive identification of potential compliance issues, allowing businesses to adjust their practices before regulatory misalignments escalate into legal challenges. On the other, they furnish entrepreneurs with strategic insights into leveraging regulatory changes as opportunities for innovation and market differentiation. The periodicity of these consultations imbues the business with a rhythm of legal introspection, ensuring that regulatory alignment is not a sporadic endeavor but a continuous thread woven into the fabric of business strategy.

In the crucible of regulatory dynamics, businesses find themselves perpetually at the cusp of adaptation, where the capacity to pivot in response to legal changes becomes a hallmark of success. This environment, marked by its constant flux, demands more than passive compliance; it calls for an active engagement with the legislative currents that shape the operational arena. The strategies delineated here, from the vigilant tracking of legal changes across jurisdictions and the leveraging of technology for efficient monitoring to the cultivation of collaborative networks and the institutionalization of legal consultations, collectively forge a comprehensive approach to regulatory engagement. This approach, rooted in proactive vigilance and strategic foresight, equips businesses to navigate the complexities of the regulatory environment with confidence, ensuring that their operations remain not just compliant but optimally positioned to capitalize on the opportunities that arise from the ever-evolving legal landscape.

7.5 Applying Business Structure Concepts to Unique Scenarios

In the intricate lattice that constitutes the decision-making process for business structures, a singular truth emerges: the path to selecting an optimal framework is not paved with uniform blocks but is a mosaic of varied scenarios, each demanding its own set of considerations. This reality underscores the necessity for a bespoke approach, where decisions are not merely reactive but are sculpted with precision to fit the unique contours of each business. The endeavor to tailor structure decisions to the specific needs and goals of the business is not just a task; it is an imperative that calls for a strategic melding of foresight, adaptability, and nuanced understanding. The influence of industry-specific considerations on structure choice cannot be overstated. Different sectors, with their unique regulatory landscapes and market dynamics, exert distinct pressures on businesses, shaping the framework within which they operate. For instance, a venture in the healthcare domain, ensnared in a web of stringent privacy regulations and liability risks, might find the protective embrace of an LLC indispensable. Conversely, a digital marketplace, thriving on agility and rapid scale, may lean towards a corporation to facilitate equity-based incentives for talent and easier access to capital markets. This alignment of structure with industry nuances ensures not only compliance but also positions the business for competitive advantage, weaving regulatory demands and market opportunities into the very fabric of its operational DNA.

As businesses evolve, the foresight to incorporate potential pivots and expansions into the foundational choice of structure becomes invaluable. The selection process, therefore, transcends current needs, projecting into the future to anticipate shifts in the business model, scale, and market engagement. A structure that offers flexibility for such evolution without necessitating frequent overhauls stands as a beacon for businesses aiming for longevity and growth. This strategic foresight allows for a fluid transition through growth phases, ensuring that the business remains agile, responsive to opportunities, and resilient against the vicissitudes of market dynamics.

Unique scenarios present themselves as crucibles for innovation, challenging entrepreneurs to venture beyond conventional structures to carve out unique advantages. The landscape is dotted with tales of businesses that, confronted with peculiar challenges or opportunities, opted for unconventional structures to leverage strategic benefits. A consultancy, for instance, might adopt a cooperative model, distributing ownership among its members to foster a culture of collaboration and align incentives, thereby enhancing service quality and client satisfaction.

Such innovative structuring requires not just a deep understanding of legal frameworks but also creativity in application, crafting bespoke solutions that reflect the unique ethos and aspirations of the business.

The tapestry of business structure decisions is a complex weave of strategic considerations, industry-specific demands, future scalability, and the innovative spirit of entrepreneurship. The endeavor to tailor these decisions to the unique scenarios faced by each business is not a linear task but a dynamic process that demands agility, foresight, and a profound understanding of both the legal landscape and market intricacies. This process, while intricate, offers a pathway to building a business that is not only compliant and efficient but also poised for growth and innovation, reflective of the unique vision and ambition that drive the entrepreneurial spirit.

In sum, the journey through the maze of business structure decisions is a nuanced endeavor, requiring a thoughtful approach that considers the unique needs, industry context, and future aspirations of the business. This chapter has illuminated the importance of customization in the selection process, highlighted the impact of industry-specific considerations, underscored the necessity for flexibility in anticipating future changes, and celebrated the innovative approaches that unique scenarios demand. As we transition from this exploration, we carry forward the understanding that the choice of business structure is a pivotal decision, one that shapes not just the operational framework of the enterprise but also its trajectory of growth and its capacity to navigate the complexities of the business landscape.

Chapter 8

Simplifying Complexities: The Essence of Business Structures

In a world teeming with infinite complexities, the allure of simplicity acts as a beacon for the weary traveler. The domain of business structures, with its intricate weave of legalities and operational nuances, often feels like a labyrinth designed for the erudite. Yet, beneath this veneer of complexity lies a fundamental truth: at its core, the choice of business structure is about aligning the framework of operation with the beating heart of the enterprise — its vision, mission, and the values it seeks to uphold. This alignment, critical for the business's survival and growth, necessitates a demystification of the jargon and complexities that shroud the decision-making process.

8.1 .Simplifying Business Structures: Beyond Jargon

Clarity and Simplicity in Explanation

In dissecting the anatomy of business structures, the first step is to strip away the layers of complexity that make these concepts appear daunting. The commitment to clarity and simplicity in explaining these concepts is not merely a pedagogical choice but a necessity. It is akin to unraveling a tightly wound ball of yarn, where each thread represents a different aspect of business structures — liability, taxation, governance, and scalability.

The process of unraveling begins with the use of everyday language, transforming abstract legal terms into digestible, relatable content. This approach does not dilute the richness of the information but makes it accessible, ensuring that entrepreneurs can make informed decisions without being hampered by the fear of the unknown.

Practical Examples and Analogies

Nothing bridges the gap between theory and understanding better than practical examples and analogies. Imagine explaining the concept of limited liability through the scenario of a ship's captain navigating treacherous waters. Just as the captain's liability is limited to the value of the ship and its cargo, so too is an LLC owner's risk confined to their investment in the business, safeguarding personal assets from business debts. This analogy not only illuminates the concept but grounds it in a scenario that is vivid and memorable, making the abstract tangible.

Visual Aids for Conceptual Clarification

The power of visual aids in overcoming the intimidation factor associated with business structures cannot be overstated. A well-designed infographic that maps out the different business structures, highlighting their key features, advantages, and limitations, serves as a visual anchor for the reader. It simplifies comparison and facilitates a deeper understanding of how each structure aligns with the entrepreneur's specific needs and goals. This visual element acts as a compass, guiding the reader through the decision-making process with clarity and confidence.

Interactive Content for Engaging Education

Interactive content, such as quizzes and decision trees, transforms passive reading into an active learning experience. Consider a digital questionnaire that prompts the entrepreneur to input specific details about their business—its size, industry, financial goals, and risk tolerance. Based on these inputs, the tool generates a recommendation for the most suitable business structure, providing a personalized analysis that resonates with the reader's unique situation. This interactive element not only reinforces learning but also makes the exploration of business structures an engaging, dynamic process.

In this chapter, the journey through the complexities of business structures is reimagined as an exploration, where clarity, practical examples, visual aids, and interactive content serve as the tools for demystification. The goal is not merely to inform but to empower, ensuring that entrepreneurs are equipped with the knowledge and confidence to choose the business structure that best aligns with their vision and operational realities. This exploration, grounded in the principles of simplicity and accessibility, seeks to transform the daunting into the doable, guiding readers through the intricacies of legal and operational frameworks with ease and assurance.

8.2   Why This Book Is Up-to-Date and Essential

In the rapidly mutating landscape of business, where legal frameworks evolve with the pace of technological innovation and market demands, the value of current, actionable information cannot be overstated.

This book stands as a testament to the commitment to delivering the freshest insights into business structures, ensuring that every piece of advice, every legal consideration, and every strategic recommendation remains relevant to today's entrepreneur. The commitment extends beyond the mere presentation of facts; it delves into the latest legal amendments, regulatory shifts, and emerging trends that influence the choice of business structure. This dedication ensures that readers are not navigating with an outdated map but are equipped with knowledge that reflects the current state of play.

Far from being a mere repository of information, this book introduces a structured approach to decision-making. It acknowledges the multifaceted challenges entrepreneurs face when selecting a business structure, offering more than just data. Instead, it provides a compass — grounded in the latest industry insights — that guides readers through the

decision-making process with a blend of analytical rigor and intuitive understanding. This unique approach does not just inform — it empowers readers, enabling them to weave through the complexities of legal, financial, and operational considerations with confidence and clarity. It recognizes that the choice of a business structure is not a decision to be made lightly; it is a foundational strategy that influences the trajectory of growth, the capacity for resilience, and the potential for innovation within the business. To maintain this book's standing as an indispensable resource in the entrepreneur's toolkit, a commitment to continuous updates cements its relevance. The digital companion to this text serves as a dynamic extension, a living document that breathes with the pulse of the business world. Here, readers find not just updates but a dialogue with the evolving narrative of business structures. Online resources, linked directly to the latest legislative changes, ensure that the book remains an authoritative source of advice, reflecting the fluid nature of business law and strategy. This commitment to ongoing relevance guarantees that readers are always a step ahead, navigating the complexities of business with the most current knowledge at their disposal.

At the heart of this book's unique value proposition are the insights from industry experts and advisors. These contributions elevate the content from informative to transformative, offering perspectives that blend theoretical understanding with practical experience. The experts, drawn from a spectrum of industries, shed light on the intricacies of business structures with a depth that only comes from first-hand experience. Their advice, rooted in the realities of managing and growing a business, provides readers with a richer, more nuanced understanding of the implications of each strategic choice. This collaboration ensures that the book does not merely present options but contextualizes them within the real-world challenges and opportunities that entrepreneurs face. It is this synthesis of expertise that imbues the book with its unparalleled value, making it not just a guide but a mentor for those seeking to navigate the complexities of business structuring with wisdom and foresight.

In the end, the essence of this book's indispensability lies not just in its adherence to current trends or its structured approach to decision-making but in its recognition of the entrepreneur's journey as one of continuous learning and adaptation. It acknowledges that the landscape of business is ever-changing, and with each shift, new challenges and opportunities arise. By providing a resource that is not only up-to-date but also rich with expert insights and structured for strategic decision-making, this book becomes an essential companion for the entrepreneur. It is a tool that not only informs but also inspires, guiding readers through the maze of business structuring with clarity, confidence, and an eye towards the future.

8.3   Industry-Specific Insights and Examples

In the vast expanse where business meets industry, the terrain is marked by distinct landscapes, each with its unique challenges and opportunities. This diversity necessitates a deep dive into the nuanced dynamics that shape structure decisions within varied sectors. The inclusion of industry-specific case studies serves not merely as an illustrative tool but as a lens, magnifying the intricate interplay between operational demands and structural frameworks.

These narratives, rich with the texture of real-world experiences, offer a mosaic of insights, shedding light on the strategic considerations that underpin the choice of business structures across different industries.

The spectrum of industries—ranging from the rapid innovation cycles of technology startups to the stringent regulatory confines of healthcare services—presents a tableau of scenarios where structure decisions can significantly influence a business's capacity to navigate sector-specific hurdles and leverage inherent opportunities. For a technology firm, the ability to swiftly adapt to market shifts and attract venture capital might steer the decision towards a corporate structure, while a consulting firm may prioritize the operational flexibility of an LLC to accommodate a fluctuating client base and project-centric work. Each case study encapsulates a strategic journey, where the selection of a business structure is not an arbitrary checkpoint but a deliberate choice, informed by an intimate understanding of industry-specific dynamics.

Tailored advice, therefore, becomes the compass that guides entrepreneurs through the decision-making process, ensuring that the choice of structure resonates with the unique characteristics and aspirations of their venture. This book's focus on offering customized solutions recognizes the diversity of reader needs, extending beyond generic advice to provide strategies that address the specific challenges and opportunities encountered within different industry landscapes. For instance, a startup in the renewable energy sector, grappling with the complexities of government grants and environmental regulations, requires guidance that is markedly different from that needed by an e-commerce platform eyeing global expansion. This tailored approach not only enhances the relevance of the advice but also amplifies its impact, empowering entrepreneurs to make decisions that are strategically aligned with their industry context and business goals.

Understanding industry trends is pivotal in informing structure choices, as these trends often herald shifts in regulatory landscapes, consumer behaviors, and technological advancements. The book's exploration of emerging industry trends delves into how these dynamics can shape the strategic terrain for businesses, influencing everything from market entry strategies to competitive positioning. For example, the burgeoning trend of sustainability and corporate social responsibility may prompt businesses in manufacturing and retail to adopt structures that support transparency, stakeholder engagement, and ethical governance. By weaving these trend analyses into the decision-making fabric, the book equips readers with the foresight to align their structure choices with both current realities and future possibilities, ensuring that their ventures are primed for resilience and growth in a rapidly evolving marketplace.

Networking and mentorship emerge as invaluable resources in this context, offering a conduit for personalized advice and support that transcends the pages of this book. The networks that entrepreneurs build within their industries serve not only as platforms for knowledge exchange but also as ecosystems of support, where shared experiences and insights can illuminate the path forward. Mentorship, in particular, offers a transformative experience, providing access to wisdom gleaned from years of navigating the industry's highs and lows. These relationships, cultivated through industry associations, networking events, and professional forums, provide a lifeline for entrepreneurs, offering guidance that is deeply rooted in the practicalities of industry-specific challenges and opportunities. By leveraging these networks and mentorship opportunities, readers can gain access to a wealth of personalized advice, augmenting the insights gleaned from this book with the nuanced understanding that comes from lived experience.

In the intricate dance between business and

industry, where each step is informed by a complex interplay of factors, the insights and examples shared in this section serve as a beacon. They illuminate the strategic considerations that underlie structure decisions, offering a window into the tailored approaches and industry-specific strategies that can propel businesses to success. Through case studies, tailored advice, trend analyses, and the leveraging of networks and mentorship, this book provides a comprehensive toolkit, empowering entrepreneurs to navigate the industry landscapes with confidence and strategic acumen.

8.4 Personalized Advice Through Interactive Elements

In a realm where business structures morph from mere concepts into the living sinews that support the aspirations of entrepreneurs, the bespoke guidance offered by interactive tools stands as a lighthouse amidst the fog of indecision. These digital architects craft pathways tailored to the individual's narrative, ensuring that the advice dispensed resonates with the unique blueprint of each venture. The interactive elements within this book, from online calculators to decision-making tools, emerge not as mere novelties but as crucial instruments, sculpting customized solutions from the raw material of entrepreneurial dreams.

The essence of these tools lies in their capacity to transform static content into dynamic interactions, fostering a dialogue between the reader and the vast expanse of knowledge encapsulated within this tome. Consider, for instance, an online calculator designed to weigh the financial implications of different business structures against the backdrop of the reader's specific fiscal landscape. This tool does more than crunch numbers; it illuminates the financial path that aligns with the entrepreneur's goals, offering clarity amidst the cacophony of tax regulations and liability concerns. Through this personalized lens, the abstract becomes tangible, and the theoretical finds its footing in the practical world.

Engagement with content, particularly when facilitated through interactive quizzes and scenarios, serves as a catalyst for deeper comprehension. Each question posed and scenario unravelled acts as a thread, pulling the reader deeper into the fabric of understanding. By placing the reader at the heart of these hypothetical situations, these tools perform a dual function. They not only test the waters of the entrepreneur's grasp of business structures but also immerse them in the complexities and nuances of each decision. This engagement transcends passive reading, morphing into an active process of discovery where each click and response carves out a deeper niche of understanding within the reader's mind.

The feedback loops incorporated within these interactive elements serve as the crucible for refining comprehension and decision-making. As the reader navigates through quizzes or utilizes decision-making tools, the feedback provided acts as a mirror, reflecting both the strengths and areas for growth in their understanding. This immediate response mechanism ensures that learning is not a one-way street but a circular journey where feedback informs improvement, and improvement fuels further exploration. It is within this iterative cycle that the true value of interactive content shines, offering not just information but a pathway to mastery.

Accessibility remains the cornerstone upon which the edifice of interactive content is built. In recognizing the diversity of experiences and backgrounds that readers bring to the table, these tools are designed with a broad spectrum of users in mind. Whether it is the fledgling entrepreneur taking their first steps into the business world or the seasoned veteran looking to pivot into new territories, the interactive elements within this book are crafted to be universally navigable. This commitment to accessibility ensures that the insights and guidance offered are not confined to a select few but are available to all who seek to demystify the complexities of business structures. The design of these tools, intuitive and user-friendly, ensures that barriers to understanding are dismantled, allowing insights to flow freely and knowledge to be absorbed without hindrance.

In the realm where theory intersects with practice, and knowledge seeks its application, the interactive elements introduced in this chapter stand as beacons of personalized guidance. They offer more than mere information; they provide a compass for navigating the choices that define the structural foundation of a business. Through tailored advice, engaging content, iterative learning, and universal accessibility, these tools embody the essence of personalized learning. They invite the reader into a dialogue, transforming the journey through business structures from a solitary trek into a guided exploration. In this landscape, where decisions ripple through the future of an enterprise, such personalized guidance is not just beneficial; it is indispensable.

8.5   The Value of a Book Over Free Online Resources

In an era where the digital expanse teems with an overabundance of information, discerning the wheat from the chaff becomes a formidable task for the modern entrepreneur. The allure of instantaneous access to a seemingly infinite repository of data, while seductive, often belies the fragmented and sometimes unreliable nature of free online resources. In contrast, the meticulously curated content of this book provides a solid foundation for decisions, standing as a bulwark against the tides of misinformation and superficial understanding that pervade the digital landscape.

The architecture of knowledge presented within these pages is not merely an aggregation of facts but a carefully woven tapestry of vetted information. Each thread, representing a core concept or strategy, is selected with precision, ensuring its relevance and accuracy. This contrasts sharply with the sprawling, chaotic web of online resources, where the provenance of information can be murky, and the veracity of content is often compromised by the absence of rigorous editorial oversight. The entrepreneur, seeking reliable insights, finds in this book a sanctuary of truth, a place where each piece of information has been scrutinized for its integrity and value.

Progressing beyond the mere presentation of information, the structured learning paths offered herein provide a coherent and guided educational experience. This structure, akin to an academic syllabus, builds knowledge progressively, introducing concepts in a logical sequence that fosters deep comprehension and retention. This methodical approach stands in stark contrast to the piecemeal and often disjointed nature of online resources, where information is scattered across disparate sources, forcing the reader to cobble together a coherent understanding from fragments of knowledge. Here, the reader is taken by the hand and led through the intricacies of business structures with a deliberate and thoughtful cadence, ensuring a holistic grasp of the subject matter.

The depth of understanding facilitated by this book transcends the superficial acquaintance with topics that characterizes much of the information found online. Through comprehensive coverage of each subject, readers gain not just a cursory familiarity with concepts but a profound comprehension that empowers them to make informed decisions. This depth is achieved through a synergy of detailed explanations, real-world applications, and expert analyses, creating a multidimensional learning experience that equips entrepreneurs with the knowledge to navigate the complexities of the business world with confidence. This richness of content, where each topic is explored with thoroughness and precision, offers an educational experience that individual online articles, with their inherent limitations in scope and detail, simply cannot match.

Moreover, the inclusion of expert insights and case studies infuses the learning experience with a layer of practical wisdom that is often absent from free online resources. These contributions, drawn from the front lines of business and academia, provide a window into the real-world application of theoretical concepts, grounding abstract ideas in the tangible realities of the marketplace. Through these narratives, readers are privy to the triumphs and tribulations of those who have navigated the path before them, gaining invaluable perspectives on the challenges and opportunities inherent in each business structure. This melding of theory and practice, enriched by the voices of experience, elevates the educational journey, transforming it from a solitary quest for knowledge into a shared exploration of the entrepreneurial landscape.

As this exploration draws to a close, the value proposition of this book emerges with clarity. In a realm saturated with information, the discerning entrepreneur seeks not just data but wisdom; not just facts but understanding. This book, with its foundation of curated, vetted information, structured learning paths, comprehensive coverage, and expert insights, offers a beacon of knowledge in the tumultuous seas of the digital age. It stands as a testament to the power of deliberate, thoughtful education, providing entrepreneurs with the tools to build not just businesses, but legacies.

As we turn the page, the narrative unfolds further, inviting readers to delve deeper into the strategic considerations that shape the destiny of enterprises. In the chapters that follow, the focus shifts to the dynamic interplay of market forces, technological innovations, and global trends, offering a roadmap for navigating the future of business with foresight and agility. This journey, rich with the promise of discovery, beckons with the assurance that the wisdom contained within these pages will light the way.

Chapter 9

Crafting Your Path: Tailored Strategies in Business Structure

In the realm of business, a well-trodden path does not guarantee the most fruitful outcome. Each entrepreneur faces a unique set of circumstances, shaped by their aspirations, market conditions, and the inherent strengths and weaknesses of their business model. Recognizing this, the strategic choice of a business structure becomes not a question of following the crowd but of charting a course that aligns closely with individual goals and operational realities. This chapter sheds light on how personalized learning paths and interactive tools can transform the daunting task of selecting a business structure into a tailored journey of strategic discovery.

9.1 Personalized Learning Paths with Interactive Tools

Customizable learning paths cater to individual needs and goals.

The digital era has ushered in an age where information is not merely consumed passively but interacted with dynamically, allowing for a learning experience that adapts to the user's pace, interests, and learning style. In the context of business structures, this adaptability is crucial. An entrepreneur in the nascent stages of formulating a business idea requires a different knowledge base than a seasoned business owner looking to pivot or scale. Personalized learning paths, therefore, offer a solution by allowing readers to navigate content that resonates with their current needs, ensuring relevance and immediacy in learning. For instance, an entrepreneur contemplating the leap from a sole proprietorship to an LLC due to growing liability concerns can find tailored content that addresses this specific transition, outlining the steps, benefits, and considerations involved.

Interactive tools facilitate applied learning.

The leap from theoretical understanding to practical application is often where learning finds its true test. Interactive tools such as online simulators or decision trees serve as bridges over this gap, offering entrepreneurs a sandbox environment to explore the consequences of different business structure choices without real-world stakes. A decision tree, for example, could guide the user through a series of questions about their business—its size, industry, financial goals, risk tolerance—culminating in a structure recommendation that aligns with their inputs. This hands-on approach not only cements understanding but also instills confidence, empowering entrepreneurs to make informed decisions rooted in a deep comprehension of their implications.

Tailored content addresses diverse business scenarios.

The diversity of the business landscape defies a one-size-fits-all approach. From the bustling streets of a metropolis where a retail startup considers the benefits of an S-Corporation to the quiet home office of a freelancer deliberating the simplicity of a sole proprietorship, each scenario demands a unique strategic approach. Tailored content that addresses these diverse scenarios ensures that no entrepreneur feels left adrift. This specificity makes the exploration of business structures not just a scholarly exercise but a practical guide, lighting the way through the fog of uncertainty that often accompanies structural decisions.

Progress tracking encourages continuous learning. The path to mastery is seldom linear, marked instead by moments of insight, revision, and sometimes, redirection. Features that enable progress tracking within the learning experience serve as milestones, offering tangible evidence of the journey's advances and the terrain yet to cover. This feedback loop, much like the progress bars in video games or the chapters in a book, provides a visual and psychological incentive to continue, transforming learning into a pursuit marked by small victories and continuous improvement. For the entrepreneur, this means not just a deeper understanding of business structures but a growing confidence in their ability to navigate the complexities of the business world.

Visual Element: Interactive Learning Dashboard

An infographic illustrating an interactive dashboard where entrepreneurs can select their learning path, access interactive tools, and track their progress. The dashboard is divided into sections, each representing a different aspect of business structure learning—fundamentals, case studies, decision-making tools—with progress bars and checkpoints that light up as the user advances through the content. This visual representation underscores the personalized, dynamic nature of the learning experience offered, emphasizing the journey's adaptability to the learner's pace and interests.

In closing, the strategic selection of a business structure, pivotal to the operational and financial success of an enterprise, demands more than a cursory understanding. It requires a deep dive into the nuances of each option, guided by personalized learning paths and interactive tools that transform this exploration into a tailored journey of strategic discovery. By offering customizable content, practical application through interactive tools, and the ability to track progress, entrepreneurs are equipped not just with knowledge but with the confidence to make decisions that best align with their unique business scenarios. This approach ensures that the choice of a business structure becomes a cornerstone in the foundation of a successful enterprise, carefully laid with the precision and insight that only a personalized learning journey can provide.

9.2   Modular Learning for Busy Entrepreneurs

In an era where the tempo of entrepreneurial life seldom slackens, the adaptability of educational content to fit into the staccato rhythm of daily commitments becomes not just beneficial but imperative. The architecture of this book, therefore, eschews the monolithic for the modular, crafting a learning experience that respects the time constraints and fluctuating focus of the modern entrepreneur. This modular structure, akin to a mosaic, allows for the absorption of knowledge in discrete, manageable segments, each self-contained yet part of a broader conceptual tapestry. It acknowledges that the pursuit of knowledge often competes with the immediate demands of running a business, offering a solution that harmonizes learning with the cadence of entrepreneurial life.

The inherent flexibility of this design caters to the entrepreneur who seeks to hone in on areas of immediate relevance. Whether grappling with the nuances of liability protection or deciphering the labyrinth of tax implications, the reader can navigate directly to the modules that address their pressing concerns. This targeted approach maximizes learning efficiency, ensuring that time invested yields direct, actionable insights. It mirrors the decision-making landscape of business itself, where focus is allocated not uniformly across all areas but strategically, to zones of immediate impact. The modular design, in this way, becomes a reflection of the entrepreneurial mindset, prioritizing areas of need without demanding a linear progression through the material.

Moreover, the utility of this structure extends beyond initial learning, supporting reference and review as the entrepreneur's business evolves. The challenges faced at the inception of a venture differ markedly from those encountered during scaling or diversification. The ability to revisit specific modules, to refresh understanding or explore previously uncharted content, provides a resource that grows in tandem with the business. It transforms the book from a one-time read into a perennial guide, its chapters revisited like familiar landmarks on an expanding entrepreneurial landscape. The ease with which one can return to particular discussions or strategies ensures that the value derived from the book extends far into the future, adapting to the entrepreneur's changing needs.

Critically, despite its segmented approach, the modular design does not fragment the coherence of the learning experience. Each module, while capable of standing alone, contributes to a cumulative understanding, building upon the concepts and strategies introduced in preceding sections. This progressive layering of knowledge, where each segment enriches and expands upon the last, fosters a deep, integrated comprehension of business structures. It mirrors the process of building a business, where each decision, each strategy, and each adaptation builds upon those that came before, driving towards a cohesive vision. The modular design, in embodying this principle, ensures that learners emerge not with scattered insights but with a comprehensive, nuanced understanding of how business structures can be tailored to their specific entrepreneurial journey.

This approach to learning, particularly suited to the restless dynamism of entrepreneurial life, mirrors the broader shifts in educational philosophy towards customization and adaptability. It reflects an understanding that the most effective learning experiences are those that mirror the realities of the learner's world, offering flexibility, depth, and relevance. In offering a modular structure, this book not only accommodates the hectic schedules of entrepreneurs but also respects the diversity of their experiences and the specificity of their needs. It is an acknowledgment that in the multifaceted world of business, a one-size-fits-all approach to learning is as ineffective as it is in business structuring itself.

The value of this approach is immeasurable, providing a scaffold for knowledge that is as robust as it is flexible, capable of supporting the entrepreneur's growth from nascent beginnings to mature operations. It affirms that the pursuit of understanding, particularly in realms as complex and dynamic as business structuring, should not require the sacrifice of other commitments but should integrate seamlessly into the fabric of daily life. This book, with its modular design, stands as a testament to the possibility of such integration, offering a beacon for entrepreneurs navigating the challenging yet rewarding waters of business creation and growth.

9.3   Continuous Learning: Beyond the Book

The pursuit of knowledge within the realm of business structures does not find its terminus upon reaching the final page of this text. Rather, the narrative crafted within these pages serves as a prologue to a richer, more expansive exploration of strategic enterprise formation and evolution. This text, while comprehensive, stands as an initial foray into a subject marked by its depth and breadth, inviting readers to extend their inquiry through a variety of conduits designed to augment the foundational understanding established herein.

The digital extension of this book, encapsulated in its companion website or application, represents a dynamic platform through which the content's value is not merely preserved but amplified. Here, the static becomes kinetic, as updated content and interactive tools breathe life into the principles and strategies discussed. The digital platform serves as a living library, where new developments, emerging trends, and pivotal legal changes are chronicled, ensuring that the entrepreneur's knowledge base remains both current and relevant. This extension transcends the conventional boundaries of a book, offering an interactive space where learning is continuous, and engagement is encouraged. Tools that simulate decision-making scenarios provide an arena for the application of knowledge, allowing users to test hypotheses, explore outcomes, and refine strategies in a controlled, risk-free environment. This digital realm thus becomes a crucible for the practical application of theoretical insights, fostering a deeper, more nuanced understanding of business structures.

Further enriching this journey is the access to networking opportunities facilitated by the book. The path of the entrepreneur, often solitary, is reimagined as a communal voyage, where experiences, challenges, and triumphs are shared. The book acts as a catalyst, connecting readers with a community of peers and experts who offer not just companionship but a wealth of knowledge and support. This network, diverse in its composition, provides a tapestry of perspectives that enrich the individual's understanding, offering insights into how different business structures are navigated across industries and geographies. Events, both virtual and physical, sponsored by the book's platform, offer venues for these interactions, fostering relationships that extend beyond professional acquaintances to become pivotal sources of support and collaboration. In this interconnected space, the value of networking transcends the mere exchange of business cards, evolving into a vital component of continuous learning and professional growth.

Integral to ensuring the content's ongoing relevance and impact is the mechanism for feedback incorporated within the book's digital platform. This feedback loop, inviting commentary and critique from readers, serves as a vital pulse check, ensuring that the book remains responsive to the needs and curiosities of its audience. Suggestions for new topics, requests for clarification, and discussions on emerging trends inform the iterative refinement of the book's content and supplementary resources. This participatory model, where readers contribute to the evolution of the narrative, ensures that the book does not remain static but grows in richness and depth, shaped by the collective wisdom of its readership. The dialogue fostered through this feedback not only enhances the book's utility but also strengthens the sense of community among its readers, creating a collaborative space where knowledge is not just consumed but contributed to and expanded upon. The ethos of continuous learning championed by this book recognizes that the landscape of business is one marked by perpetual change. Legal frameworks evolve, market dynamics shift, and strategic paradigms are redefined, necessitating an approach to learning that is both adaptive and proactive. The book, in offering pointers to further resources, courses, and materials, serves as a guidepost, directing readers to avenues through which their exploration of business structures can continue to deepen. These resources, carefully curated, represent a spectrum of knowledge that complements and expands upon the foundational understanding established within these pages. From specialized courses that delve into the intricacies of tax law to seminars on leadership and organizational design, the recommended materials offer pathways for intellectual expansion and skill development. This holistic approach to learning, encompassing both the theoretical underpinnings of business structures and the practical skills required for their effective implementation, ensures that the entrepreneur is not just well-informed but well-equipped to navigate the complexities of the business world.

In this landscape, where change is the only constant, the book emerges not as a final destination but as a departure point, inviting readers to embark on a journey of continuous learning and adaptation. Through its digital platform, networking opportunities, and feedback mechanisms, the book extends its reach beyond the printed page, offering a dynamic, interactive space where knowledge grows, evolves, and thrives. This approach, recognizing the multifaceted and ever-changing nature of business, ensures that readers are not just equipped with a static set of insights but are empowered to engage with the subject matter in a manner that is reflective, responsive, and perpetually enriching.

9.4   Real-Time Updates: Staying Current

In the ever-shifting sands of the business landscape, where regulatory frameworks and market dynamics evolve with relentless momentum, the imperative for entrepreneurs to remain abreast of these changes cannot be overstated. This necessity transcends mere academic interest, embedding itself as a cornerstone of strategic agility and operational compliance. The fabric of this book, while rich in foundational knowledge and strategic insights, is augmented significantly by its commitment to providing real-time updates through an array of online resources. This commitment is not a cursory nod to the digital age but a deep-seated acknowledgment of the fluid nature of business law, regulation, and strategy.

The realm of subscription services and memberships emerges as a pivotal element in this ecosystem of continuous learning. These platforms, intricately linked to the book's core content, serve as conduits for the flow of up-to-the-minute information on shifts in business structures, legal amendments, and strategic innovations. Imagine, if you will, a service meticulously curated to align with the thematic pillars of this book, offering not just updates but a contextual analysis of how these changes impact various business structures. This service, accessible through a subscription model, ensures that readers are not merely informed of developments but are equipped with the knowledge to navigate their implications. Each update, delivered with precision and clarity, is designed to integrate seamlessly with the foundational knowledge imparted by the book, ensuring a coherent and comprehensive understanding of both current states and emerging trends. Alerts and notifications stand as the sentinels in this landscape of continuous information. Through the strategic use of email alerts or app notifications, readers are kept informed of critical developments that bear significance to their interests and operations. This feature, far from being an intrusive barrage of information, is calibrated to the specific interests and preferences of the reader. Whether it is a groundbreaking legal ruling that alters the liability landscape for LLCs or a tax reform that impacts S-corporations, these alerts ensure that such pivotal information reaches the reader with alacrity, enabling timely responses and strategic adjustments. The elegance of this system lies in its customization, allowing entrepreneurs to filter the flow of information to match their unique business scenarios and structural considerations.

Within the vibrant forums and discussion boards that accompany the book's online platforms, an intricate tapestry of community contributions unfolds. Here, readers from diverse industries and regions converge, bringing with them a wealth of perspectives and insights. This communal pool of knowledge, enriched by the varied experiences of its contributors, serves as a living repository of strategy, challenges, and innovation. Contributions from a reader navigating the regulatory intricacies of launching a startup in Asia offer as much value as insights from a seasoned entrepreneur expanding their operation across Europe. This diversity of perspectives not only broadens the reader's understanding but also fosters a sense of global community, bound by the shared pursuit of entrepreneurial excellence. The book, in facilitating these exchanges, extends its role from a source of knowledge to a platform for dialogue, where the diversity of experiences enriches the collective wisdom.

This model of continuous updates, supported by subscription services, alerts, and community contributions, reflects a broader vision. It encapsulates a commitment to ensuring that the strategic choice of a business structure, a decision foundational to the success and sustainability of an enterprise, is informed by the most current and relevant information. This approach acknowledges the dynamic interplay between legal frameworks, market conditions, and strategic planning, offering entrepreneurs a compass by which to navigate these complexities. It is an acknowledgment that in the world of business, where change is the only constant, staying informed is not just a strategy but a necessity.

9.5   Inclusive and Diverse Perspectives in Business

Within the vast expanse of the business world, the mosaic of experiences paints a picture far richer than a monochromatic canvas could ever convey. It is in this diversity of voices, each narrating a tale of triumphs and trials, that true wisdom and innovation are birthed. This book, in its exploration of business structures, pledges allegiance to this diversity, ensuring that the tapestry of perspectives it presents is as varied as the entrepreneurs it seeks to guide.

Diverse Business Experiences Enrich Understanding and Innovation

The acknowledgment that no two entrepreneurial journeys mirror each other underpins the narrative woven throughout these pages. From the bustling markets of Lagos to the tech hubs of Silicon Valley, the challenges encountered and the solutions crafted bear the imprint of their environment. It is through the lens of these varied experiences that the book draws its strength, offering not just a guide to business structures but a window into the myriad ways these frameworks can be navigated. The inclusion of case studies from a spectrum of business owners — each with their unique approach to overcoming obstacles — ensures that the reader finds resonance, regardless of their geographical location or industry.

Inclusion Promotes a Broader View of Potential and Challenges

The challenges faced by underrepresented groups in the business arena often go unnoticed in mainstream discourse. This book aims to rectify this oversight by shining a spotlight on the unique hurdles encountered by women, people of color, and other marginalized entrepreneurs. Through targeted advice and solutions, it seeks to level the playing field, offering insights that are not just generic but cognizant of the specificities that shape these entrepreneurs' experiences. This focus not only enriches the reader's understanding but also fosters a sense of inclusivity, ensuring that the narrative is reflective of the diverse tapestry of the business world.

Global Perspectives Offer a Wider Lens on Business Structures

The exploration of business structures cannot be confined to a single geographical context. The global economy, intertwined and interdependent, demands a broader outlook. By incorporating case studies and insights from across the globe, the book transcends borders, offering readers a panoramic view of how different cultures, legal systems, and market dynamics influence the selection and navigation of business structures. This global perspective broadens the reader's understanding, illuminating the fact that the principles governing business structures are not insular but universal, albeit colored by local nuances.

Collaborative Learning Fosters Empathy and Innovation

The ethos of collaborative learning permeates the narrative of this book, championing the idea that collective wisdom far outweighs individual insight. By encouraging dialogue among readers from diverse backgrounds, the book becomes more than a repository of knowledge — it transforms into a forum for exchange. This interaction not only fosters empathy, allowing readers to step into the shoes of others with differing viewpoints but also catalyzes innovation. The cross-pollination of ideas, germinated in the fertile soil of diverse experiences, promises solutions that are not just creative but also inclusive, reflective of the multifaceted nature of the business landscape.

In stitching together this rich tapestry of perspectives, the book does not merely inform — it transforms. It challenges the reader to view the selection of a business structure not as a solitary decision but as one influenced by a kaleidoscope of factors — cultural, social, economic. It invites them to see beyond the confines of their immediate environment, to consider how the same principles apply in different contexts, and to learn from the experiences of those who might walk a different path but share the same destination.

This exploration, while rooted in the specifics of business structures, extends its tendrils into broader themes of diversity, inclusion, and global interconnectedness. It underscores the notion that in the realm of business, as in life, perspective is everything. The ability to view challenges through the lens of others, to understand the nuances that shape decisions in different environments, enriches not just our approach to business but our approach to problem-solving and innovation.

As we turn the page, leaving behind the vibrant mosaic of experiences and insights that have colored our exploration of business structures, we carry forward the understanding that diversity is not just a buzzword — it is the bedrock of innovation. The lessons gleaned from this chapter, reflective of the broader tapestry of the business world, serve as a foundation upon which future strategies can be built. In recognizing the value of varied perspectives, in understanding the global context within which business operates, and in fostering a culture of collaborative learning, entrepreneurs are better equipped to navigate the complexities of the business landscape. This understanding, while marking the end of one chapter, lays the groundwork for the next, promising a journey that is not just informed but transformative.

Chapter 10

Navigating the Future: Business Structures in Flux

In the tapestry of business, each thread—be it economic, technological, or societal—interweaves to create a landscape that is both vibrant and volatile. The choice of a business structure, then, is not a decision etched in stone but a strategic pivot point, susceptible to the winds of change. As the world whirls around, propelled by innovation and transformation, the astute entrepreneur recognizes the imperative to remain not just informed but ahead, anticipating the shifts that will inevitably color the horizon of business structuring.

10.1   Emerging Trends in Business Structures

The landscape of business structuring does not exist in a vacuum; rather, it pulsates with the rhythm of economic, technological, and societal trends. The rise of digital enterprises and the burgeoning field of social entrepreneurship are not merely blips on the radar but harbingers of a paradigm shift in how businesses are conceived, constructed, and cultivated.

Adaptability is Key to Navigating Future Changes

The hallmark of a resilient business structure is its adaptability to future trends and market shifts. Consider the digital enterprise, its very essence rooted in the fluidity and flexibility of the internet age. A business model that once might have thrived as a brick-and-mortar establishment now finds its optimal structure in the virtual realm, untethered by the constraints of physical space, yet bound by the need for cyber security and data protection. This shift necessitates a business structure that can pivot with agility, embracing the digital frontier while safeguarding its assets against the unique vulnerabilities of the online world.

Innovative Structures May Offer New Advantages As the landscape evolves, so too do the structures that underpin business operations. Decentralized autonomous organizations (DAOs) and hybrid models emerge from the crucible of innovation, challenging traditional norms and offering a glimpse into the future of collaborative enterprise. DAOs, operating on blockchain technology, democratize decision-making, removing hierarchical barriers and dispersing authority among its members. This structure, reflective of the ethos of the digital age, prioritizes transparency, collective governance, and a shared vision, presenting an intriguing alternative to the conventional corporate model.

Regulatory Evolution Will Impact Structure Decisions

The fluidity of business structures is mirrored in the evolution of regulatory frameworks that govern them. As new models like DAOs gain traction, regulatory bodies are prompted to reconsider existing statutes, paving the way for legal reforms that accommodate these innovative structures. Proactive planning becomes essential for businesses, as staying abreast of potential regulatory changes can mean the difference between compliance and conflict. For instance, a business contemplating a transition to a DAO model must navigate not just the technological implications but also the legal landscape, ensuring its operations align with emerging regulations and standards.

Visual Element: The Evolution of Business Structures Infographic

An infographic detailing the evolution of business structures captures the transition from traditional models to innovative alternatives like DAOs and hybrid organizations. This visual narrative, with its timelines and trend lines, illustrates the impact of economic, technological, and societal shifts on business structuring, providing a concise yet comprehensive overview of the past, present, and future.

In the realm of business, change is the only constant, a principle that underscores the strategic selection of a business structure. The entrepreneur, then, must not only navigate the present landscape with acumen but also cast an eye toward the horizon, anticipating the shifts that will shape the future of business structuring. The adaptability of a business structure, its alignment with regulatory evolutions, and its openness to innovation form the pillars upon which long-term success is built. In this dynamic environment, the entrepreneur's ability to foresee, adapt, and innovate becomes not just a strategy but a survival mechanism, ensuring that the business not only endures but thrives in the flux of the future.

10.2 Technological Innovations Impacting Business Operations

The relentless march of technology reshapes landscapes with an impartial hand, where the realm of business operations and structures is no exception. In this era, propelled by an inexhaustible engine of innovation, the very bedrock upon which enterprises stand finds itself under a constant state of flux. Blockchain and artificial intelligence (AI), once nestled within the confines of speculative fiction, now punctuate the strategic dialogues of boardrooms with their transformative potential. These technologies, in their nascent yet potent form, extend an invitation to businesses to reconceptualize operations, partnerships, and the foundational structures that underpin their existence.

Blockchain, with its promise of decentralized and immutable ledgers, offers a glimpse into a future where transactions, contracts, and records transcend the traditional paradigms of trust and verification. The implications for business structures are profound, enabling models where operational transparency and stakeholder trust are not just aspirational goals but embedded characteristics. Consider a scenario where supply chains, often mired in opacity and inefficiency, are revitalized through blockchain's transparent and verifiable records, enabling businesses to streamline operations and forge trust with an increasingly conscientious consumer base. The ripple effect extends to intellectual property management, where blockchain's capability to ensure the provenance and ownership of digital assets empowers creators and innovates the economics of content distribution.

Simultaneously, artificial intelligence ushers in an era of unprecedented operational efficiency and predictive prowess. AI's capability to analyze vast datasets and glean actionable insights allows businesses to anticipate market trends, tailor customer experiences, and optimize supply chains with a precision hitherto unattainable. This technological boon, however, necessitates a reevaluation of business structures to accommodate the integration of AI-driven

decision-making processes, ensuring that the architecture of businesses is conducive to the infusion of these intelligent systems. The alignment of business structures with AI's capabilities becomes a strategic imperative, fostering environments where data-driven insights inform strategic decisions, from product development to market entry strategies.

The digital transformation that envelops the modern enterprise is not merely a transition to online platforms but a redefinition of how businesses operate, engage with customers, and pursue growth. This transformation influences business structuring at a fundamental level, particularly concerning operational efficiency and global reach. The adoption of digital platforms enables businesses to transcend geographical constraints, opening avenues to global markets with a fluidity that challenges traditional business models. This global digital presence requires structures that support agility, allowing businesses to navigate the complexities of multiple regulatory environments and cultural landscapes. The imperative for operational efficiency, magnified by the global scale of digital enterprises, calls for structures that leverage digital tools for process optimization, customer engagement, and innovation incubation.

In this digital epoch, the paradigms of collaboration and partnership undergo a metamorphosis, facilitated by technology's capacity to connect, communicate, and co-create across distances. The traditional barriers that segmented businesses and isolated expertise dissolve, giving way to models of partnership that are dynamic, distributed, and digitally native. These models, underpinned by platforms that enable seamless collaboration, challenge the conventional frameworks of joint ventures and alliances, advocating for structures that are flexible,

project-based, and oriented towards shared goals. This new form of collaboration, buoyed by technology, not only expands the scope of potential partnerships but also redefines the mechanisms through which these partnerships are forged and fostered. Amidst these opportunities, the specter of data privacy and cybersecurity looms large, casting a shadow over the digital transformation narrative. The increasing reliance on digital platforms and the proliferation of data as a strategic asset amplify the importance of cybersecurity measures within business structures. Companies, especially those whose operations are intricately tied to digital platforms, find themselves at a crossroads where the integration of robust cybersecurity protocols into their structural DNA is not optional but essential. This integration extends beyond mere compliance with data protection regulations, evolving into a strategic differentiator that signals trustworthiness to customers and resilience to stakeholders. The decision-making matrix for business structuring thus expands to include considerations of data privacy and cybersecurity, ensuring that the architecture of businesses is fortified against the vulnerabilities inherent in a digitally interconnected world.

In the dance of technology with business, where every step forward reshapes the floor upon which the next will be taken, businesses find themselves in a perpetual state of adaptation. The innovations that define this era — blockchain, AI, digital transformation — serve not just as tools for operational enhancement but as catalysts for structural evolution. They challenge businesses to reimagine their foundations, to construct structures that are resilient, adaptive, and aligned with the technological zeitgeist. In this reimagining, the entrepreneur acts not merely as a spectator but as a sculptor, molding the enterprise with an eye towards both the present capabilities and the future potentials of technology.

10.3 Global Perspectives on Business Structuring

In the intricate web of modern commerce, globalization acts as both a catalyst and a crucible, reshaping the domain of business structuring with an unrelenting force. This phenomenon, characterized by the flow of goods, services, capital, and knowledge across borders, has significantly widened the horizons for entrepreneurs seeking to establish or expand their ventures. The impact of globalization on business structuring is profound, compelling a reevaluation of traditional models in light of the complexities and opportunities inherent in a globally connected market.

The influence of globalization on business structuring is multifaceted, encompassing the need to navigate a labyrinth of international laws and market dynamics. Entrepreneurs venturing beyond domestic confines must contend with a patchwork of regulatory environments, each with its distinct legal frameworks governing corporate conduct, taxation, and intellectual property rights. This legal pluralism demands a strategic approach to structuring, where decisions are informed not only by the potential of foreign markets but also by the imperative to comply with a diverse array of laws and regulations. The choice of structure, thus, becomes a balancing act, weighing the benefits of global expansion against the complexity of operational compliance in multiple jurisdictions.

Cross-border operations, while fraught with challenges, present a landscape rife with opportunity. The intricacies of managing a business that straddles multiple countries include not just the negotiation of varied tax regimes but also the cultivation of multinational partnerships.

These alliances, often forged within the crucible of shared goals and mutual interests, offer a conduit for navigating the complexities of international commerce. They provide a platform for sharing risks, pooling resources, and leveraging local expertise, thereby enhancing the competitive edge of businesses on the global stage. However, the formation and management of these partnerships hinge on a nuanced understanding of cultural norms and business practices, underscoring the importance of cultural intelligence in global operations.

Cultural considerations, in this context, transcend mere etiquette, permeating deep into the strategic fabric of business structuring. The alignment of business practices with local cultures is not an exercise in tokenism but a strategic imperative that influences every facet of operations, from marketing and customer engagement to human resource management and dispute resolution. Businesses that adeptly navigate these cultural landscapes can harness the full potential of international operations, transforming cultural diversity from a hurdle into a strategic asset. This cultural attunement fosters not only smoother operations but also deeper connections with local markets, enhancing brand resonance and customer loyalty across diverse demographic segments.

The strategic advantages of international networks and collaborations are manifold, extending beyond the immediate benefits of market access and risk diversification. These networks serve as vital arteries, pumping the lifeblood of innovation, knowledge, and capital throughout the global body of the enterprise. They facilitate the exchange of ideas and best practices, enriching businesses with a wealth of perspectives that spur innovation and drive competitiveness.

Furthermore, these collaborations act as buffers against the volatility of global markets, offering stability in the face of geopolitical shifts and economic fluctuations. The strategic structuring of businesses to optimize these international networks and collaborations is not a mere tactical choice but a foundational strategy that can significantly influence long-term success in the global marketplace.

In the vast expanse of global commerce, where opportunities and challenges coalesce, the strategic structuring of businesses emerges as a critical determinant of success. Entrepreneurs, armed with a keen understanding of international laws, cultural nuances, and the dynamics of cross-border operations, can navigate the complexities of globalization with confidence. This navigation, informed by a strategic approach to business structuring, transforms the potential pitfalls of global expansion into stepping stones, paving the way for businesses to thrive in the interconnected markets of the modern world.

As we conclude this exploration of global perspectives on business structuring, the key themes resonate with clarity. The impact of globalization demands a strategic reevaluation of traditional business models, emphasizing the importance of adaptability, legal compliance, and cultural intelligence. The opportunities presented by cross-border operations, coupled with the strategic advantages of international networks and collaborations, underscore the potential for businesses to not just survive but flourish in the global marketplace. This foray into the complexities and opportunities of global business structuring sets the stage for a deeper dive into the strategic considerations that shape the destiny of enterprises in the chapters that follow.

Conclusion

As we draw the curtain on this explorative journey through the multifaceted world of business structures, let's pause and reflect on the path we've traversed together—from the foundational understanding of various business structures to the nuanced exploration of their legal, financial, and strategic dimensions. This journey, layered with complexities, has been demystified, transforming confusion into clarity, apprehension into assurance, enabling you, the reader, to navigate the decision-making process with informed confidence.

The essence of our exploration underscores the criticality of selecting an appropriate business structure. It's not merely a procedural step but a strategic decision that influences legal protection, tax obligations, operational nimbleness, and the potential for scalability. The knowledge imparted here aims to fortify your decision-making arsenal, ensuring that choices are not made in isolation but are aligned with a comprehensive understanding of each structure's impact on liability, funding avenues, taxation, and growth trajectories.

Empowerment and confidence have been central themes, with the intent to equip you, especially if you're at the beginning of your entrepreneurial journey, with the confidence to discern the business structure that best suits your venture's vision. This confidence is cultivated on a bedrock of knowledge, elucidating how strategic alignment with long-term goals, operational efficiency, and market positioning can significantly influence your business's resilience and adaptability.

Now, the baton is passed to you. Armed with this knowledge, I encourage you to delve deeper, engage with professionals, and utilize the tools and resources presented throughout this guide to refine your understanding and choice of business structure. This is not the end but a beginning—the commencement of a strategic, informed, and confident phase in your entrepreneurial journey.

I invite you to connect with me on social media platforms, where the dialogue continues, enriched by updates, shared experiences, and the collective wisdom of a community of like-minded entrepreneurs. Your feedback on this book, your stories of navigating business

structures, and your questions are not just welcome; they are invaluable. They contribute to a dynamic ecosystem of learning, adaptation, and growth.

In the ever-evolving landscape of business, change is constant, and so is learning. Stay curious, remain open to new insights, and be ready to pivot in response to the shifting sands of the business environment, regulatory frameworks, and market needs.

As we part ways, remember that entrepreneurship is a journey marked by challenges, learning, and growth. The road ahead may be fraught with uncertainty, but armed with the right knowledge, preparation, and strategic choices regarding your business structure, you are well-equipped to navigate the path to success. Let the insights from this book be your compass, guiding you through decisions that not only shape your business today but pave the way for its flourishing future. Here's to you, to the ventures you will build, and to the impact you will create. May your entrepreneurial journey be as rewarding as it is successful.

With every good wish for your journey ahead,

DA Affiliates 2,

References

- *How To Start A Sole Proprietorship (2024 Guide)*
  https://www.forbes.com/advisor/business/how-to-start-a-sole-proprietorship/

- *Pros and Cons of a Limited Liability Company (LLC)*
  https://www.investopedia.com/articles/investing/091014/basics-forming-limited-liability-co mpany-llc.asp

- *Compare Types of Partnerships - LP, LLP, GP*
  https://www.wolterskluwer.com/en/expert-insights/compare-types-of-partnerships-lp-llp-g p

- *The Benefits of an S Corp (Plus the Disadvantages) Explained*
  https://www.goldenappleagencyinc.com/blog/s-corp-benefits-and-disadvantages#:~:text= As%20a%20certain%20type%20of,that%20must%20be%20carefully%20followed.

- *LLC vs. Corporation: How Are They Different? (2024) - Shopify*
  https://www.shopify.com/ca/blog/llc-vs-corporation

- *Business structures | Internal Revenue Service*
  https://www.irs.gov/businesses/small-businesses-self-employed/business-structures

- *How to protect your intellectual property | LegalZoom*
  https://www.legalzoom.com/articles/how-to-protect-your-intellectual-property

- *How To Change Your Business Entity*

https://www.rocketlawyer.com/business-and-contracts/starting-a-business/legal-guide/ho w-to-change-a-business-entity

- *Choose a business structure* https://www.sba.gov/business-guide/launch-your-business/choose-business-structure

- *LLC vs. Corporation - What is the difference between an ...* https://www.mycorporation.com/learningcenter/llc-vs-corporation.jsp

- *The Financial Risks And Uncertainties Of Owning A Small Business* https://www.forbes.com/sites/melissahouston/2023/09/17/the-financial-risks-and-uncertai nties-of-owning-a-small-business/

- *Business structures | Internal Revenue Service* https://www.irs.gov/businesses/small-businesses-self-employed/business-structures

- *How Strategy Shapes Structure* https://hbr.org/2009/09/how-strategy-shapes-structure

- *LLC or Corporation: What Is Best for Your New Business or ...* https://founderslegal.com/llc-or-corporation-what-is-best-for-your-startup/#:~:text=LLCs%20offer%20more%20flexibility%20and,too%20rigid%20for%20some%20businesses.

- *7 Successful Business Pivot Examples - WDHB*

- https://wdhb.com/blog/7-business-model-pivots-you-can-learn-from-d721cbfbea36/ *Impacts of Government Regulations on Businesses* https://sanctionscanner.com/blog/impacts-of-government-regulations-on-businesses-312

- *Successful Entrepreneurs Who Started Out As Sole Proprietors* https://www.gaebler.com/Successful-Entrepreneurs-Who-Started-Out-As-Sole-Proprietors.htm

- *Startup Success Stories: How LLCs Paved the Way for ...* https://www.personalbrandingblog.com/startup-success-stories-how-llcs-paved-the-way-f or-unicorns/

- *Strategic partnerships: Lessons from the field – Case studies* https://www.cpacanada.ca/business-and-accounting-resources/strategy-risk-and-govern ance/strategy-development-and-implementation/publications/strategic-partnership-series -introduction/strategic-partnerships-case-studies

- *How to Create a Startup Growth Strategy* https://www.embroker.com/blog/startup-growth-strategy/

- *Legal Terms Every Entrepreneur Should Know* https://blog.goodlawyer.ca/goodlawyer-blog/legal-terms-every-entrepreneur-should-know

- *Choose a business structure* https://www.sba.gov/business-guide/launch-your-business/choose-business-structure

- *Business structures | Internal Revenue Service* https://www.irs.gov/businesses/small-businesses-self-employed/business-structures

- *Business Law Today from ABA | Issues, Articles - Insight You ...* https://businesslawtoday.org/

- *Single-Member LLC vs. Sole Proprietorship - Wolters*

Kluwer https://www.wolterskluwer.com/en/expert-insights/singlemember-llc-vs-sole-proprietorshi p

- *LLC pass-through taxation: What small business owners need to know* https://www.wolterskluwer.com/en/expert-insights/llc-pass-through-taxation-what-small-b usiness-owners-need-to-know#:~:text=Pass%2Dthrough%20taxation%20means %20that ,tax%20on%20any%20remaining%20revenue.

- *How To Change Your Business Entity - Rocket Lawyer* https://www.rocketlawyer.com/business-and-contracts/starting-a-business/legal-guide/ho w-to-change-a-business-entity

- *Top Tools for Regulatory Compliance* https://visualping.io/blog/top-tools-monitor-regulative-intelligence-compliance/

  - *Business Entity Comparison Chart - PublicLegal* https://www.ilrg.com/corp/entitycomparison.html

- *Small Business In 2023: Experts Predict Trends And ...* https://www.forbes.com/sites/allbusiness/2023/01/1 6/small-business-in-2023-experts-pre dict-trends-and-challenges/

- *Legal Graphics: Present Your Argument With Compelling Visuals* https://courtroomanimation.com/legal-graphics-present-your-argument-with-compelling-vi suals/ *15 Free Online Learning Sites Every Entrepreneur*

Should ... https://www.entrepreneur.com/living/15-free-online-learning-sites-every-entrepreneur-sho uld/238908

- *Individual Personalized Learning - ERIC* https://files.eric.ed.gov/fulltext/EJ1275355.pdf
- *The 10 Best Business Intelligence Tools For Decision-Making* https://datarundown.com/business-intelligence-tools/

- *Why Being A Lifelong Learner Is Essential For Entrepreneurial Success* https://www.forbes.com/sites/forbesbusinesscouncil/ 2023/09/29/why-being-a-lifelong-lear ner-is-essential-for-entrepreneurial-success/

- *The Business Case For Diversity is Now Overwhelming. ...* https://www.weforum.org/agenda/2019/04/business-case-for-diversity-in-the-workplace/

- *The 5 Biggest Business Trends In 2023 Everyone Must Get Ready For* https://www.forbes.com/sites/bernardmarr/2022/10 /03/the-5-biggest-business-trends-for- 2023/
- *The impact of blockchain technology on business models* https://link.springer.com/article/10.1007/s12525-019-00386-3

- *The Impact of Globalization on Corporate Legal Structures* https://www.linkedin.com/pulse/navigating-global-waters-impact-globalization-corporate

- *The Impact Of Digital Transformation On Business Models* https://www.forbes.com/sites/bernardmarr/2023/10 /12/the-impact-of-digital-transformatio n-on-business-models-opportunities-and-challenges/

Made in the USA
Monee, IL
07 July 2026

56545978R00098